BE GOOD
THE ALLEN LUND STORY

BE GOOD
THE ALLEN LUND STORY

JENNA DAY

A NOTE FROM THE FAMILY

"Monday Night Therapy." This became the name affectionately bestowed on our weekly meeting with Jenna. After getting everyone online, unmuted, and past the laughs and jokes, Jenna would get us focused, begin asking pointed questions, and patiently listen to us with sincerity and curiosity that made us want to continue talking for hours. A few weeks into this new routine, any initial doubts we had about tackling a book project would shift to feelings of excitement, gratitude, and the realization the Holy Spirit was guiding us along the way.

Jenna, you never met our dad, but you took what was in our hearts and minds and thoughtfully weaved them into the chapters of this book. We are so grateful to you for your gift of storytelling and the care you put into every page.

Tom Romano, you were the spark that set things in motion the day you invited David, Kenny, and Eddie to lunch shortly after our dad passed away. As his close friend, often talking to him daily, you were able to impart your wisdom to us that it would be important to the employees of Allen Lund Company to know the namesake of their company and the man who was able to impact so many lives.

We appreciate the many friends, family, and ALC employees who took the time to share memories of our dad. Without these stories, this book would not have been possible.

Bishop Matt, your fingerprints are on this book in the same way you touched our dad's heart with your steadfast friendship. Your guidance and support have been a true blessing in our lives.

Mathew Kelly and Dynamic Catholic, thank you for believing in our dad's story. We couldn't think of a better partner to have as our publisher. We are grateful to be a small part of your "mission to create resources to inspire people to rediscover Catholicism."

Mom, although this book is about Dad, it is really about the life you built together. We've cherished the opportunity this book created to reminisce, laugh, and cry with you each week. We love you and are inspired by you every day. Also, thank you for only choosing to remember the positive things we did as kids!

Dad, we miss you every day, and through these pages, we hope to honor your life, your faith, and your legacy. We are proud to share your story and pray that everyone who reads this book will be enriched with lessons from a life well lived. We love you and we will never forget what you taught us—work hard, be good, and go to Mass.

David Lund
Natalie (Lund) Peterson
Kenny Lund
Eddie Lund
Anna (Lund) Clapp
Christina (Lund) Doerfler

wellspring

Copyright © 2025 Jenna Day
PUBLISHED BY WELLSPRING
AN IMPRINT OF VIIDENT

ISBN: 978-1-63582-586-2 (hardcover)
ISBN: 978-1-63582-587-9 (eBook)
Audiobook available from Audible

Design by Maggie Barnett

10 9 8 7 6 5 4 3 2 1

FIRST EDITION

Printed in the United States of America

TABLE OF CONTENTS

For the employees of Allen Lund Company:

"The greatest employees in the world"
—D. Allen Lund

ACKNOWLEDGEMENTS

Writing a book about a man as wonderful and inspiring as Allen Lund has been one of the greatest honors of my life. I am infinitely grateful to my fearless editors, Bill Swinford and Tom Moran. Your red ink, honesty, and encouragement elevated this text to soar far above my own capabilities. I would like to thank the Lund Family for trusting me with your Father's story. Thank you for patiently enduring my endless questions and for the bravery and vulnerability you brought to our meetings each week. Also, thanks for taking me to The Patio in Blanding, Utah. To date, it's still the best milkshake I've ever had. To Anthony Preston, thank you for introducing me to this project. It is no small undertaking to organize and disseminate information spanning the scope of a life as large as Allen's. In many ways, your work canvased and graded the land on which the foundations of this book were laid. Your respect for Allen Lund was palpable when you first spoke to me about him, and I am forever grateful for your contributions to this project. I am profoundly appreciative of everyone who was interviewed. Your stories helped shape my understanding of Big Al. I was able to know him by the fingerprints he left on you.

Allen, studying your life has changed mine. My hope is that

this story will impact readers in a similar way. If Heaven ever updates its logistics from fiery chariots to supernatural semi-trucks, I'd like to put in a request for a ride, but only after I've attempted to run a race as faithful as yours.

Finally, thanks be to God. You work all things out for the good of those who love You. You hear our prayers and direct our steps. May this book glorify You and lead many to find peace and courage in Your beautiful life-giving Presence. I love you, Lord Jesus, with all my heart.

FORWARD

"We are never completely ourselves unless we belong to a people. That is why no one is saved alone, as an isolated individual. Rather, God draws us to himself, taking into account the complex fabric of interpersonal relationships present in a human community."

—*Pope Francis*

A person's call to holiness is both mysterious and unique. It evolves over time through each person's unique human condition. It follows the spiritual adage, "Grace builds on nature."

This call to holiness knows no vocational boundaries. Indeed, it is universal in scope. As Christians, it is grounded in the Sacrament of Baptism. The pouring of the water symbolizes the outpouring of the Holy Spirit, calling the individual to a prophetic life of spreading the Gospel of Jesus Christ.

We often hear the words "baptism by fire." This expression describes a person who experiences something in a very sudden, risky, and intense way that challenges the person to quickly adapt and prove him/herself. Allen Lund experienced his "baptism by fire" at nineteen years of age. It sowed the seeds of a nascent belief in God. A couple of years later, it would germinate through the Sacrament of Baptism through a special relationship with "Her."

As Pope Francis writes, "We are never completely ourselves unless we belong to a people….no one is saved alone…God draws us to himself through relationships." Indeed, we are called to holiness by building the Kingdom of God on earth, by enriching the lives of people through the gifts that God has given uniquely to each of us. Allen Lund, through his Baptism by Fire and the Holy Spirit, was infused with an understanding of this beyond natural means – indeed, it was truly supernatural.

A "Renaissance Man" of keen intellect, superb intuition, well versed in topics far and wide – and without a college education – Allen grasped that his Baptism would call him to create a community of love and well-being for everyone. It would begin with his marriage to his wife, Kathie and the creation of their family. With time, it would spread like wildfire in the development of a national corporation and again, in the tangible fortification of Catholic institutions, parochial and educational.

Allen Lund got it! One's salvation is not an individual experience, rather, it is borne through the creation of communities that reflect our Baptismal call, namely, ones that work to reflect the unity of the Blessed Trinity – the perfect community of love.

Be Good: The Allen Lund Story reminds us that we are all called to holiness through the gift of Baptism. We are all called to be "saints."

Pope Francis in his apostolic letter, *Rejoice and Be Glad* writes, "There are heroic people, hidden saints who belong to the 'middle class of holiness' that you do not see but they are there." The "middle class of holiness," as defined by Francis, is composed of people who are "heroic in their everyday life, seeking the good of others and in this way, finding their own good."

Accordingly, whether married or divorced, single or separated, Baptism challenges each of us to grow in holiness through the daily, ordinary, humble practice of our own vocation. This was and will always be, Allen Lund.

Our call to holiness deepens as we grasp the essence of our Baptism. Holiness reaches a pinnacle when we come to know how much we are loved by God – that is, unconditionally. This love is not earned or some "payment plan" for what God has done for us over our lifetime. This unconditional love is re-discovered when we reach this point in our spiritual life. Allen came to a profound understanding of this later in life; it was experienced through tears of joy that streamed down his face.

Allen's journey is our journey. In the words of Pope Benedict XVI, "We become ourselves only to the extent that we acquire the ability to acknowledge others." This comes through God's grace.

Our call to holiness is mysterious and unique. Grace builds on our human condition.

"Just be yourself, everyone else is taken."—Oscar Wilde

Bishop Matthew G. Elshoff, OFM Cap.
Auxiliary Bishop, Archdiocese of Los Angeles
and Allen's Friend of 30 Years

CHAPTER ONE

BORN FROM THE ASHES

"Be who God meant you to be, and you will set the world on fire."
—*St. Catherine of Siena*

A pillar of smoke rose from the mountains and smeared the western horizon with ominous clouds of ash. The thick stratus was illuminated red by the bright flames ravaging the earth below. At a distance, the employees of Foss Lewis Sand and Gravel watched as the wildfire consumed the foothills of the Wasatch Mountains that bordered Bountiful, Utah. The climate made the area susceptible to wildfires, and 1959 had been an unseasonably dry year. The fire spread quickly over the parched earth, creating one of the biggest blazes in Davis County history.

There was no rain in the forecast and high speed winds continued to fuel the flames. Hundreds of residents were without power and the firefighters weren't able to maintain their firelines because their engines couldn't make it up the steep ridges of the mountainous terrain.

Foss Lewis was the largest heavy machinery construction company in Bountiful, Utah. Armed with their arsenal of earth moving equipment, the employees of Foss Lewis had been called upon to help overwhelmed local firefighters. The men stood at attention in their well worn work boots and dusty blue jeans awaiting instructions.

Among this ragtag group of volunteers stood nineteen-year old Allen Lund. He listened carefully as the foreman explained the gravity of the situation. Allen may have been one of the company's younger employees, but he had quickly earned a reputation for being competent and trustworthy. The foreman gave Allen specific instructions. Allen was to take a bulldozer up the mountain and rescue some stranded firemen whose fire-engine got stuck on the ridge. The rest of the men would start reinforcing firelines on an adjacent ridge.

Allen grabbed a chain and headed for his Caterpillar bulldozer. He had been given a tremendous responsibility. The stakes were high and he would be on his own for this assignment. For many teenagers this task would be overwhelming, but life had already equipped Allen with a profound self-sufficiency and unique set of hard skills that set him apart from his peers.

As early as five years old, Allen Lund's grandfather started teaching him how to operate heavy machinery and farm equipment. His father also made a career as a big rig driver. Young Allen Lund had a natural aptitude for this type of work. He could operate anything with an engine, something that quickly made him stand out as Foss Lewis' best equipment operator.

It didn't take Allen long to get up the ridge and find the firetruck lodged in the slippery terrain. Allen connected the fire engine's rear axle to the hitch on his bulldozer and climbed back aboard the thirty-thousand-pound steel beast. He engaged the throttle and nervously watched the chain tighten. This was the moment of truth. Allen didn't know if he could dislodge the fire engine from the landscape before the torque of the bulldozer ripped its axle out from under it. He cringed with each new screech of the fire engine's contorting chassis. Finally, the engine's spinning wheels found traction, and it slowly lurched from the steep quagmire to freedom.

Relieved, Allen shut down the bulldozer, wiped his brow, and gazed upon the darkened Utah sky. Ash cascaded like snow and the smokey air stung his nostrils. The firemen shook Allen's hand. They were grateful to be freed but disheartened by how powerless they felt in this battle against the spreading fire.

Their engine simply would not make the climb up the ridge to cut a new fireline in that location, so they decided to head back down and find a different place to fortify against the flames. Thanking Allen again, the firemen climbed aboard their dislodged engine and carefully navigated their way back down the mountainous slope. Before departing, they warned Allen he should do the same.

Allen could see a new flank of flames in the distance, leaping down the eastern ridge of the foothills of the Wasatch Mountain like a game of hopscotch. If it continued to spread in the same direction it would be on a collision course with a neighboring subdivision. If the wind carried on, these homes would be lost and many families would be displaced.

Allen raised his arms, flexed his hands back, and cocked his head to the side. Closing one eye, his sightline traced down his arm as if he were looking down the barrel of one of his hunting rifles. His hands were like iron sights. He was using his body as a plumbline to study the terrain, something he had done countless times while ascertaining how to grade golf courses, roads, and foundations for Foss Lewis.

Allen had fulfilled the assignment his employer asked him to do. He was supposed to return after freeing the firemen. However, Allen wrestled with the feeling he had just been handed a second mission that day. No one could tell him what to do. Allen was alone on the ridge and knew he had a decision to make. The firemen may not have been able to make it further up the ridge, but Allen believed he could. He knew he had the skill and means to intervene, but he would be taking a huge risk.

Through squinted eyes, he considered the terrain once more.

"Well it's the right thing to do now, isn't it," he whispered to himself before climbing back on the bulldozer. His gaze and resolve were fixed on the burning ridge. He engaged the throttle and drove toward the flames.

In 1958, Caterpillar dozers had a top speed of 20 miles per hour; and did not benefit from modern tools like air-conditioned cabs, geographic navigational equipment, and lidar scanners that map topography. There were no drones to view burn areas or monitor hot spots for future flare-ups. Allen Lund was operating on sheer will, natural instinct, and a talent forged in him by his father and grandfather when he was a child. He could use the mechanical arms in such a way that they would almost be an indistinguishable extension of his own. All he had on that mountain ridge was natural talent and guts. All he could make was an educated guess about the landscape. All he knew for sure was that he would do whatever he could to prevent lives from being lost and save homes from being destroyed. It was simply the right thing to do.

When he arrived at the perimeter of the subdivision, he lowered the bulldozer's boom and thrust its blade into the ground, sending dirt, sand, and foliage flying into the air. Throwing the Caterpillar into reverse, he started cutting a fire line several yards wide and just deep enough into the soil to remove any flammable material that would feed the fire. This would form a protective trench to keep the fire at bay. Back and forth he dug, as far as he could, violently bouncing around the Caterpillar like a man in the belly of the beast. He struggled against the twisted topography as burning debris poured down all around him.

In the midst of battle and without warning, the wind picked up, aggressively funneling the fire towards him. Within seconds, daylight became like night as a wave of black smoke consumed the area. Allen shifted the dozer into gear and plotted his escape. He barreled down the hillside with searing heat at his back. Before he could arrive at a safe distance, the bulldozer began to choke on the smoke-filled, oxygen-depleted air. It staggered to a halt.

He had gotten himself into a bad situation. He was trapped and would be unable to outrun this fire. The stakes were now life or death, and he needed to think quickly. In addition to his deftness with heavy machinery, Allen had a creative streak to his problem-solving. He was fortunate to have this talent, because in the middle of the chaos he had a moment of life-saving inspiration.

Allen thrust the blade of the dozer back into the earth. He feverishly ripped a small trench a couple of feet wide and a few feet deep as the heat began to scorch his skin. He parked the dozer over the freshly dug trench and left just enough space for himself to climb below the machine. Allen burned his hands on the searing metal as he leaped from the suffocating dozer and squeezed beneath it, burying himself in the soft clay earth– just as the fire consumed everything around him. The roar was as deafening as a jumbo jet. The smoke was blinding. The heat was unbearable. Allen pushed his burnt hands deep into the soil until his fingers found plant roots and he gripped them for dear life.

With his eyes shut and teeth gritted, he tried to avoid panic by occupying his mind with images of pleasant times. He thought about his two younger sisters. He thought about the cool marble floors he admired in the bank where his mother worked as a loan officer. As the hellish fire raged around him, Allen prayed to a God he wasn't sure existed, begging to be spared. He bargained with this God to save his life, promising to devote it to helping others with every waking, smoke-free breath from that day on. Seconds felt like an eternity. Allen kept time by counting the exploding hydraulic lines on the bulldozer. They blew up one by one with loud bangs, an ominous metronome. Steam began to rise from the soil as the heat evaporated the moisture in the ground. Struggling to breathe and boiled in immense heat, Allen began to lose consciousness. He grappled for one thing to fixate on to keep himself awake. With each fleeting breath, gripping the roots so hard his knuckles turned white, he clung to the memories he had of *her*.

CHAPTER TWO

GREENER GRASS

"Up to a point a person's life is shaped by environment, heredity, and changes in the world about them. Then there comes a time when it lies within their grasp to shape the clay of their life into the sort of thing they wish it to be."

—Louis L'Amour

The man forged in the fires of the Davis County blaze miraculously survived that night, emerging stronger. He put himself in harm's way because in his mind it was simply the right thing to do. That inner compass is what Allen Lund would build his life on. It's what buried him in the earth that night. Though unbeknown to Allen, that burial was like a seed that would bring forth a mighty harvest, and no one looking at the life of Allen can deny the enormous yield and legacy he built in his seventy-seven years on the Earth.

Looking at the lives of great men and women teaches and inspires us to take great action in our own lives. That is certainly the case when observing Allen Lund, a giant of a man whose name most people have never heard, but who impacted the lives of so many. As a businessman, he transformed the logistics and transportation industry, built a company that recently surpassed 1.4 billion dollars in annual revenue, and became a beacon of light in his community through his many philanthropic endeavors. In spite of all this, Allen referred to himself as "just a truck driver." It was this down-to-earth-no-nonsense quality that made Allen Lund unique among his peers, and this is also why simply listing his extensive accomplishments would be an insufficient audit of his life.

To understand what made Allen Lund the man he was, one must understand the calibration of that inner compass: a life aimed to honor his Creator, love his family, and help as many people succeed as he could.

Allen became a great man of faith, generosity, and industry. Yet just like a mighty oak starts with a tiny seed, he also started from humble beginnings. Nestled between the Wasatch Mountain Range to the east and the Great Salt Lake to the west is the quaint town of Farmington, Utah where Allen grew up. It occupies an area approximately 10 square miles. David Allen Lund was born here on September 3, 1940, the oldest of three children to his parents David Wayne and Maxine Lund. His younger sister, Katie, was four years younger than Allen, and the baby of the family, Judy, was twelve years his junior.

As the only son, there was enormous pressure on Allen to grow up quickly, honing skills that could serve his family. Allen's father was a complicated man, but he made sure his son became skilled with heavy machinery. Allen's father was a truck driver but also took various odd jobs around town when he could find them. He taught his son the ins and outs of excavators, bulldozers, and dump trucks—skills Allen would use for years to come.

Though most of Allen's hard technical skills came from observing his father, Allen's sense of discipline and work ethic came from his mother. Maxine Lund was the more stable care-taker of the family. She worked for over forty years at the same bank as a loan officer. However, her salary alone wasn't enough to support the family. Finances were always tight. In his early life, Allen was constantly scrambling for odd jobs, preparing for the moment his family would need his income to sustain itself.

At various points in Allen's childhood, he worked as the town dog catcher, he raised rabbits to sell, he picked fruit at an orchard. He also worked in the town cemetery. While working there, he had yet another job working for a company called Weber Water, a farmer co-op for irrigation. From 1:00 a.m. to 4:00 a.m. Allen would divert water to the cemetery, then divert it back to the cherry orchard he was also in charge of watering. Allen realized he could manage more properties by subletting his jobs, so he hired young kids in town to take over some of his duties. Gifted with the power of delegation at an early age, Allen knew that if he wanted to multiply his time and his income, he needed to multiply himself. He understood the principle of working hard, but he embraced the principle of working smart. As a result, the cemetery never looked as well-maintained as it did when Allen was in charge.

Unfortunately, Allen's forward-thinking bumped up against some of the old-fashioned ideas of a few residents in his small town. The city council felt that if they were paying him, they should have a say in his schedule. When they confronted Allen about not always being at work, he responded, "The grass is the greenest it's ever been."

"Yes it is, but we need you there all of the allotted time," one council member protested.

"Well, then I quit," Allen retorted.

To Allen, this demand was nonsensical. It was the very definition of someone cutting off their nose to spite their face. It was clear twelve-year-old Allen was precocious and ahead of his time. He was often mistaken for being older than he was, and his height allowed him to work jobs beyond his years. This expanded his ever-evolving skills and consequently matured him even faster. After quitting at the cemetery, Allen needed a job. So in 1957, two years before he would begin employment as a equipment operator for Foss Lewis, Allen Lund was employed as a ride operator at Lagoon Amusement Park, one of the oldest, family-friendly amusement parks in the United States. Lagoon is a labyrinth of lush gardens, park rides, and beautiful columned picnic pavilions overlooking stunning mountainscapes. It also possesses an iconic wooden roller coaster and picturesque sprawling pools, making it an ideal summer spot.

Located in Farmington, Lagoon drew crowds from the urban hub of Salt Lake City to its south. At the time, it was only open from Memorial Day to Labor Day each year. So it was the ideal place for a Farmington teenager to work during the summer. For Allen, it was also the perfect place to work if you didn't have the money for a season pass.

At the start of every summer, workers and some of the male high school students would come into Lagoon and test ride the old wooden roller coaster that had been dormant all winter. The coaster needed to be ridden all day long and monitored with an oil can until the track was well lubricated, and no longer rusty. On and on they rode, but it wasn't just recreation. Allen and his friends would have to push the car up the tracks and then jump in quickly to ride the coaster down the hills, and then repeat the process many times until everything ran smoothly. After days of testing and inspection, Allen and his young colleagues folded up their street clothes for the summer and donned their name tags and blue theme park uniforms.

Lagoon provided two important functions for Allen. The first was consistent summer employment. Allen seemed to be working nonstop, as his father's employment became increasingly inconsistent. Allen was incessantly haunted by the idea that his family might not have enough resources. So a summer job became vital.

The second—and equally meaningful—function Lagoon served was some decompression from Allen's home life. The jovial smiling faces of the park patrons always lifted his spirits. Allen also had a mischievous streak, which he put to good use when he was stationed to work in the funhouse that had a maze of spinning floors and wonky mirrors. The attraction had air jets that sent sudden bursts of compressed air up the vents in the floor. Young ladies in skirts would perform their best Marilyn Monroe impression, mimicking her iconic move made famous in The Seven Year Itch, a film that had exploded at the box office three years prior.

Allen would perch inconspicuously on the control platform which was hidden behind a double mirror. From there Allen could see the guests coming through the attraction, but they couldn't see him. He would blast unexpecting park patrons with the air jets as they weaved through the maze.

The Park's patrons loved Allen. He could push the rides more than the other operators because he understood the machinery safety limits. Certain rides at Lagoon would twist, spin, or invert people more than others. Allen was egged on by his regular riders to jostle them around until they experienced the full thrill of the ride. Allen loved providing folks with excitement, so he ran the rides at top speed. This simultaneously would cause money to fly out of the patrons' pockets. After a ride, Allen would often find coins just sitting on the roller coaster's seats or under the tilt-a-whirl. All he needed to do was turn the machines around and all sorts of loose items would turn into spoils for his coworkers. Allen would mark this as his very first entrepreneurial venture.

In addition to operating some of the more intricate rides, Allen's job also included being a bouncer for some of the musical acts that came through Lagoon. His tall stature made him a perfect candidate for this job. Allen was able to hear some of the most famous acts of the day including Red Nickels And The Five Pennies, and the illustrious Johnny Cash, who Allen suspected was inebriated most of the show. His role as Lagoon security also included accompanying the cashiers to the accounting office at the end of each night, looking out for everyone's safety and well-being since Lagoon was a cash only operation at that time.

One fateful night, while chaperoning the cashiers to the vault, Allen Lund met that special "her."

CHAPTER THREE

HER

"Do not despise these small beginnings, for the Lord rejoices to see the work begin."

—*Zechariah 4:10*

Life is a string of seemingly ordinary moments, the value of which is difficult to ascertain in the present. Yet viewed through the rear-view mirror of our lives, we find upon reflection that some of the most ordinary days were really quite extraordinary after all. Allen had no clue that one average summer night, among a backdrop of Lagoon's large wooden roller coaster, rides, and game booths, he would meet the great love of his life.

Her name was Kathleen "Kathie" Baranski, but almost immediately after meeting her, Allen dreamed of the day he could change her last name to Lund. He eventually succeeded in doing this on July 16, 1960, and would consider this the greatest honor of his life. Kathie and Allen would be married fifty-seven years, have six children and twenty-two grandchildren; and at the time of Allen's death they were blessed with two great-grand-children. The pair built an extraordinary life together.

It's easy to see why Allen Lund fell in love so quickly. There is something special about Kathie Lund. She is beautiful but has a radiance that's more than skin-deep. Her very soul seems to be steeped in goodness with a potency that can be felt. She speaks softly and sweetly in a way that makes you want to lean in more closely to listen to her, careful to catch every word. Friends of the Lund family frequently acknowledge there would be no Allen without Kathie. In many ways, Kathie's constant support, goodness, and faith were the keys that helped Allen become the man he was. Kathie, however, always felt like she was the fortunate one on that first summer night.

Kathie reminisces about the early days with Allen from their house in Pasadena. She has lined the halls with family photos and memorabilia that mark the wondrous journey she and Allen took together. It's a visual look in their rearview mirror, charting a journey so saturated with divine providence, intervention, and answered prayers that it would challenge the resolve of the most devout skeptics. The home, and the people inside, also exude a grounded quality that points to starting humbly and building a life up from the lowest foundations.

Kathie's humble beginning started in Layton, Utah. Kathie's biological father, Edward Victor Baranski, husband to Kathie's mother, Madeline Mae Cleary, died heroically in World War

II. He was an OSS officer and one of thirty-one American servicemen executed in a German concentration camp. This made Kathie and her younger brother Gerald—whom everyone called "Jerry"—war orphans. Kathie's mother and grandmothers rarely spoke about Edward. Their grief was enormous, and discussing him was painful. However, throughout her childhood Kathie always believed her father watched over her from Heaven like a guardian angel.

As reparations for the loss of their loved one, the government provided children of deceased veterans a small living stipend. Their mother used this stipend to fund their education. She enrolled Kathie and Jerry in a local Catholic school. This gave Kathie, and later Allen as well, a passion for Catholic education. Kathie's family resided in Layton, but she and her brother commuted to St. Joseph's Elementary School 17 miles north in the town of Ogden. Between school and her family's involvement in their local parish–St. Rose of Lima– Kathie received a solid Catholic upbringing. She was surrounded by a strong faith-filled community of friends and mentors that shaped her character and filled her childhood with some beautiful memories.

During this time Kathie also met June Letchenberg at school. June came from a Catholic upbringing and grew up in East Ogden. Having lost her mother when she was in grade school and barely seeing her father who was a traveling musician, June and her brother John bounced around within the foster care system.

June credits her strength for getting through this trying period to the special gift that God gave her: Kathie Baranski. Although their lives were different, June and Kathie had many things in common and became fast friends and kindred spirits. Every day after school, Kathie and June would have a little tea party, with tea and hot milk. The old lady who took June and her brother in was from England, so although it wasn't fancy, they felt chic drinking tea in proper British fashion. June's bedroom was partitioned with a curtain because John slept on the other side, and the girls would spend hours in there talking and laughing. The laughter was a potent medicine that helped both girls endure the ups and downs of their early adolescent years.

The friends took care of each other. June spent her upbringing in survival mode, constantly trying to adapt to new environments. Her deep friendship with Kathie provided something stable she could count on. Kathie's mother had also modeled generosity to June. When packing Kathie's lunch for school she would often sneak in extra food for June. Kathie's grandmother even gave June a prom dress when her foster family couldn't afford one. Giving freely and loving people well were hallmarks of the Baranski home.

June and Kathie were inseparable. The two peppy teens joined the cheerleading squad together, donned their knee-length felt poodle skirts with starched petticoats, and rehearsed their dance moves in the church basement. They blared musical tunes like

Billy Haley's "Rock Around The Clock" and danced to their heart's content, flipping and whipping each other around, careful to dodge the basement's support pillars.

No one in town could match their ability to have a good time, but it wasn't just fun and games that connected these friends. They also shared a common thread of authentic faith that made their friendship deep and enduring. Both girls held the strong conviction that faith was more than just words you uttered or prayers you repeated. The Holy Cross nuns at their school gave them a good foundation, teaching them scripture and instilling values of kindness, love, and service. However, the two friends were committed to building on this foundation in their everyday lives.

"You can learn the Ten Commandments, but if you don't share the relationship with Jesus that's supposed to come out of them, they're just words," June said. "We were taught to bring people *to* Jesus, to love them, to use the education of the virtues, not just the facts, to help others live better, to put that faith into action."

As iron sharpens iron, so one believer sharpens another. Having a friendship built on faith helped Kathie and June navigate high school and everything that comes with it, including dating. Over the years many suitors showed interest in Kathie. However, June prayed that Kathie would find a man worthy of her; a special man who modeled the same virtues that Kathie excluded so exquisitely.

June thought, "Kathie deserves such a man."

* * *

To get to school, Kathie took "the Bamberger Trolley." The rail line connected northeastern Ogden to Salt Lake City. It passed through Layton and Farmington, Utah, on the way to Salt Lake City. The Lagoon became the Bamberger's principal source of revenue. While Kathie and Jerry were at St. Joseph's—Kathie in third grade and Jerry in first—they convinced their mother, who worked at Hill Air Force Base, that they were old enough to ride the trolley to school by themselves.

The two were already pretty independent. Their mother had to leave for work early in the morning and wasn't able to see them off to school. However, they got to the trolley station by riding tandem on a bicycle each day. Kathie, the bossy older sister, would occupy the seat with a foot on one of the pedals, and Jerry would balance himself with one foot on a peg near the rear axle and his other foot on the free pedal.

Together they would each pump with one foot, pedaling in unison to the station and catch the trolley to school. They looked out for each other. So for only ten cents, they persuaded their mother to let them take the Bamberger Trolley from East Ogden south to Farmington and swim in some of Lagoon's freshwater lakes. Had Kathie and Jerry not been attending St. Joseph's via the trolley, it may not have ever occurred to them to visit Lagoon, and it may not have ever inspired her to want to work there.

Kathie's steps always seemed to be guided from above. Little moments and everyday people would shape the trajectory of her life. Many people in her community would become role models she would soon pattern her life after. Glen, an eighth grader Kathie admired, was always kind to everyone on the trolley ride to school. Being one of the older kids, he looked out for the younger ones. He also went to Mass every day and carried a prayer book with him everywhere he went. Inspired by his devotion, she decided to redesign her little prayer book with a white cover, put her name on it, and started carrying it with her to Mass. Like the schoolmates she admired, Kathie cultivated the habit of attending Mass each day.

As Kathie walked to church, about a mile in each direction, she passed the farm and large house of Mrs. Green who was always outside working, but she never hesitated to stop and say hello to Kathie. One day, when Kathie was sixteen, Mrs. Green asked Kathie about her plans for the summer.

"I don't know," Kathie replied, "Maybe I'd like to work at Lagoon."

"Well I know people there," Mrs. Green responded. "Maybe if we went there, I could help you get a job."

Mrs. Green spoke to Kathie's mother and got permission to drive Kathie to Lagoon. Kathie suspected that the "people" Mrs. Green knew might have included one of the Lagoon owners. As a result, Kathie was hired that same day in the early summer of 1958 and did not discover until years later that she had bypassed the waitlist of hundreds of applicants that Lagoon receives each year.

She was handed an incredible opportunity, but it took her a while to find her niche on the property. On the first day, they put her in charge of the ring toss game, but she didn't have a knack for it and didn't make her daily quota. Kathie needed something slower-paced where her diligent and methodical brain could be better utilized. They eventually made her a ticket booth cashier; a position in which she excelled. She soon earned the trust of Lagoon management who increased her responsibilities around the park. Kathie would rotate stations throughout the park, giving breaks to other cashiers working various rides. Eventually she was placed in charge of directing employee break times and closing out receipts.

Kathie was a natural. One day, while strolling through the rides at the park, she spied a tall, good-looking young man she had never seen before. He stood out to Kathie, seeming more mature than the other guys, both in manner and stature.

That evening, just like every other night, after the park closed Kathie and the other cashiers were accompanied by guards to the office to count money, roll coins, complete the accounting protocol, and put everything in the safe. On this particular evening, when exiting the office, there was a new escort waiting for her. It was the young man she'd spotted earlier. Allen introduced himself with a warm smile.

As they walked, Allen's eyes were fixed on her. He hastened to keep in step with her brisk pace. Like a magnet drawn to another, Allen instantly wanted to be right next to her.

He was entranced and nervous but attempted to sound casual when he invited her to hang out with a group of friends after work. Allen's words came out jumbled because he was starstruck.

This was endearing to Kathie who turned to face him. He looked intently at her.

Kathie wanted to know the plan. After a moment she replied, "What's open?"

"At this time? Absolutely nothing," he said with a sterling smile. Allen hadn't yet made a plan, he just knew he wanted to spend time with her. There was something in his smile that captivated Kathie and would continue to for all the years to come. In that moment, they locked eyes and felt the incandescent joy of an ordinary day becoming extraordinary.

Kathie replied, "Good enough for me."

CHAPTER FOUR

WITNESSING LOVE

"The taste of love is sweet, When hearts like ours meet, I fell for you like a child, Oh, but the fire went wild."

—*Johnny Cash*

1958 was an eventful year for Allen and Kathie. Among the tantalizing attractions and thrilling rides, a quiet and steadily blooming love story began. Their admiration and affection for each other just felt natural to them. It peacefully progressed throughout the year until it became apparent to them they had each found their forever person. Allen and Kathie had a lot in common; and their long-time childhood friends bore witness to their blossoming love and marveled at how quickly the two seemed to fall together. Kathie had June, who prayed often for the right man for her beloved friend. Allen had Ralph Wilcox, affectionately known as Arf, who understood him more than just about anyone else.

Ralph and Allen first became friends in kindergarten. Neither of them had a very traditional childhood because they were both working from a young age. Allen was working jobs for his father, while Ralph grew up on a farm where there were always more chores to do than there was time to play. This made Ralph and Allen the two de facto lone wolves in grade school, and that became their shared bond. The duo looked like young caricatures of Abbott and Costello. Even at a young age, Allen was tall, broad, and imposing. Ralph, in contrast, was petite and therefore counted on Allen's stature to deter bullies. They had a lighthearted rapport and would often tease one another. However, at the end of the day, they always stood up for the other, each in their own way. Allen defended Ralph from bigger kids who tried to pick on him, and Ralph saw a side of Allen people often overlooked.

The double-edged sword of Allen's stature was that people always thought he was older and treated him as such. When Allen and Ralph were ten years old, their Cub Scout troop went to Salt Lake to see a movie. Back then, anyone under the age of twelve would be admitted for free.

"Uh, that boy's not under twelve years of age," the ticket booth clerk said to their Cubmaster while staring at Allen.

Ironically, Allen was actually the youngest of their whole group, spawning a heated argument outside the movie theater. The embarrassing scene dragged on as the clerk simply would not admit Allen without proof from his birth certificate. Eventually, the scoutmaster paid the difference, but Ralph noticed tears quietly streaming down his best friend's face. He knew Allen didn't have it easy at home. There was enormous pressure on Allen to be the man of the house, as his father, Wayne, a functioning alcoholic, struggled mightily. In many ways, his childhood was cut short because the circumstances demanded he grow up so quickly.

Ralph knew that the father-son trips Allen would take with Wayne, which most people regarded as "so special," were quite the opposite. Ralph knew Allen didn't learn to drive tractor-trailers because of his father; he learned despite him. On one occasion, when Allen was ten, his father took him along for one of his odd jobs. They took a trip to drop off supplies three hours north. However, before making the trip home, his father stopped at a bar and drank himself into an inebriated stupor. Ten-year-old Allen drove the truck the entire three hours home.

Allen believed if he didn't figure out how to shift that 16-gear over-under transmission on his own, his father, who was passed out in the passenger seat, would thrust him, his mother, and two younger sisters into starvation.

It was this same boy who stood outside of the movie theater that night, simply wanting to feel like one of the other kids. So being publicly denied entry in front of his friends stung, and the tears didn't go unnoticed by the friend who knew him best.

Allen and Ralph attended the same schools from elementary

through high school. They were partners on the Davis High School debate team. They also dabbled in sports, though there was a limit on the number of extracurriculars in which they had time to participate. Allen was always working and Ralph could relate. Ralph grew up on a dairy farm, and could barely get away from the cows for which he was responsible. The family dairy farm was 2.5 miles away from where Allen grew up. Come rain or shine, Ralph was up every morning and out every night milking those cows.

The copious amount of work put a damper on the social lives of these two industrious teens. Allen did go out for sports. He had the ideal physique for football, but a broken leg in his first season caused him to lose his appetite for the sport altogether. He spent a semester of school on crutches, but the two friends had a way of staying on the sunny side of life by finding creative ways to have fun wherever and whenever they could. There was a kid in their class who had polio and walked with crutches. Ralph remembers numerous occasions when Allen would race the kid down the halls of the school—the battle of the crutches.

Allen and Ralph continued like Butch Cassidy and the Sundance Kid all through high school. Although Ralph said Allen would hang out with some of the guys in their class here and there, neither had much time for a social life. They also didn't have time or the know how to date anyone.

Allen worked at Lagoon for the first time in the summer of

1957 after his junior year of high school. He returned after his senior year in 1958. Ralph worked at Lagoon as well. New hires at the time had to start with sanitation duties. Ralph was part of the 5:30 a.m. clean-up crew that picked up trash and used a fire hose to wash down the pavement. These efforts ensured the park looked immaculate every day it opened.

Allen was able to bypass the clean-up crew induction due to his proficiency with heavy machinery. In true Allen Lund form, he took every opportunity to tease Ralph about it. Eventually, Ralph was promoted to Rides Manager, which technically made him Allen's new boss.

"Arf, come here, I gotta tell you something," Allen said while dumping into Ralph's hands the pocket full of loose change he had picked up from under the rollercoaster.

"Why do I get the feeling this is a bribe of some kind?" Ralph jested. Ralph was used to Allen normally being a composed and confident guy, but he was acting downright sheepish.

Allen finally came right out with it. "I met this girl…"

June and Ralph marveled at how quickly Kathie and Allen became instant friends. But there was much they had in common: similar backgrounds, experiencing the absence of their biological father in one way or another, and trying to be good examples for their younger siblings. One thing that June observed about Allen the first time she met him was that he was not braggadocious. He didn't seem to try to impress Kathie with witty banter or material possessions. June saw other suitors come around her friend, but both girls felt Allen was "the real deal." He didn't try to impress. He didn't condescend to make himself look intelligent. He wasn't a people pleaser. He was authentically himself, and he laughed loudly alongside all of them. June also observed how Allen always pushed others to the forefront, always highlighting the gifts and accomplishments of others while he tried to cloister himself in the background. It was as if he was compensating for his imposing physical presence. Whatever the case, June saw it as the model of a great leader, someone who would one day build something tremendous, and most important, someone deserving of her friend. .

Kathie and Allen complemented each other. He was a free spirit, something that allowed Kathie the safe space to relinquish control. On the other hand, Kathie had a grounded quality in her faith that brought balance and stability to Allen.

It wasn't long after they met that Allen introduced Kathie and Jerry to his sisters, Judy and Katie. The families hung out together that summer and became close. The Lagoon work schedule was six days on, so each employee upon being hired was asked what day of the week they wanted off. Kathie of course chose Sundays so that she was able to maintain attendance at Mass. Allen was intrigued by Kathie's devotion to her Catholic faith and appreciated how important it was to her, so he used his clout as Lagoon's best ride operator to get Sundays off as well. They began attending Mass together.

As the summer of 1958 drew to a close, Allen knew Kathie was the woman with whom he wanted to spend the rest of his life. He set out to become the man worthy of her hand in marriage. Allen had already graduated from high school and Kathie was about to start her senior year. He joined the Army Reserves and was stationed at Fort Ord in the coastal city of Monterey, California. There he was assigned to work on seagoing vessels. Despite the distance, he and Kathie maintained regular contact, writing letters to each other every week. Active duty lasted six months, and he was finally able to return to Farmington that Christmas of 1958. He would remain in the Reserves for the next nine years.

Allen's mother, Maxine, called Kathie asking if she wanted to accompany the family to the train station to greet Allen and welcome him home. When Allen stepped foot onto the platform, he walked straight to Kathie as if everyone else was invisible. He wrapped his huge arms around her and squeezed her into the biggest bear hug of her life.

"I remember feeling guilty that he ignored them all," Kathie recalled years later. "It was then I realized this was real. It was also something that was so telling to his family. Everything else was a blur except for that hug."

The two reignited their courtship, and Allen was more

enamored with Kathie than ever. On one of their dates, he was so lost in Kathie's eyes that when he went to pour them water from a pitcher he completely missed the glass, soaking the table and her in the process. He was silly in love. Allen was tall, mature, and confident but would melt around Kathie. Allen knew he wanted to put a ring on her finger, and with Kathie's college plans on the horizon, he wanted to do it soon. He saved the money, and in May of 1959 he presented her with an emerald-cut solitaire ring.

"Absolutely not," Kathie's mother Madeline emphatically stated as she snatched the ring out of her hand. "You're not old enough."

Madeline then placed the ring atop the windowsill above the kitchen sink—perhaps not the safest place to store it—where she claimed it would stay until Kathie turned eighteen at the end of June that year. Luckily she only had to wait four weeks to rescue the ring from the windowsill. Allen tried to get insurance on the ring, but he wasn't able to do so. The jeweler wouldn't insure it because Kathie was going to college out of state. Yet for Allen, Kathie having the ring before she left for college was an insurance policy all on its own. He wanted to lock her in before she left.

Kathie's family still felt their daughter was too young to be engaged. She had just graduated from high school. They adored Allen but felt they both lacked the life experience necessary to get married and start their life together. Allen was striving to prove himself to Kathie's family and show he could take on more responsibility. He had started working for Foss Lewis, and the job allowed him to start saving up for a life with Kathie.

It was a season of obstacles for Allen. Not only did he face pushback from Kathie's parents, but Kathie also expressed concerns about their relationship for the first time. Although Allen and Kathie continued to spend time together, she maintained her independence. She maintained it so well, in fact, that Allen claims she never officially said "yes" to his marriage proposal. Kathie claims she never said "no." But she admitted that she did say she had "never really thought about marrying someone who wasn't Catholic."

Allen's background was completely void of religious practice. His mother was a non-practicing Lutheran, and his father was a non-practicing Mormon. As far as what denomination of faith Allen Lund was, according to Kathie, he was essentially nothing. Allen Lund, a master problem solver, a man that no ship or earthmover could intimidate, a man who had succeeded in taking care of his family while his father wrestled his own demons, now found himself with a new formidable opponent: God Almighty.

Obstacles continued to mount even after Kathie turned eighteen. Kathie had been accepted into Gonzaga University in Spokane, Washington—over 700 miles from Farmington.

Despite the proposal and her love for Allen, Kathie left Ogden in the fall of 1959 for Gonzaga. The distance was hard, but it never deterred Allen.

Allen was so determined to make their relationship work in fact that not even job-related injuries could hamper his goal of turning Kathie Baranski into Kathie Lund. One day while using a backhoe to trench a basement, the radiator exploded and burned him badly with scalding water. Instead of going to the hospital, he went home to Maxine, his mother. He knew if he went to the hospital, the doctor would spend all day lancing the blisters on his skin. He didn't have time for that. As Maxine bandaged him up, she asked why he had not gone to the emergency room. Allen replied, "Trying to get married, Mom… gotta get back to it."

Meanwhile, Kathie took honors courses at Gonzaga. Years later when reflecting on her time in college, Kathie says she majored in growing up and minored in taking responsibility. The time away gave her a chance to stretch her independent spirit, but she stayed in contact with Allen every week. They would take turns calling one another. Five dollars in change would get them just a little bit of time as Kathie would spend every Sunday night racing across the University quad to get to the cafeteria in time to grab Allen's call on the pay phone. Some Allen Lund Company personnel would say later that this—along with the expense of phone calls back then—was the reason the Lund family members had a habit of ending phone conversations so quickly. This was something for which Allen became notorious.

The holidays came and went that year with lightning speed, and after a blissful time, Kathie returned to school for the second semester of freshman year. After a beautiful Christmas and ringing in the New Year, Kathie felt excited to start planning a life with Allen. She loved him and respected him, and she believed God would work out the rest. Allen attended Mass with Kathie. He was very supportive and interested in her faith, but he still wasn't where she was on the topic. However, Kathie wasn't worried. She confidently trusted God could take a spark of faith and fan it into flame in Allen's heart. She hoped and believed that God would be the Father to Allen that his biological one never was. She prayed that something would ignite in his life; a spark or even just an ember that would give him the passion to pursue faith the way she had.

As Kathie prayed for a spark, God delivered a blazing fire.

* * *

Steam rose from the fire-scorched ground. The earth as far as the eye could see was as black as the sky, the lingering smoke blending the horizon between them both. The once deafeningly loud environment of the violent flames was now deafeningly quiet. Nothing moved. After a while, something eventually stirred. A hand, black and red with brown fingernails, emerged from the ground. More dirt began to budge, until finally, Allen Lund crawled out from beneath his Caterpillar like Lazarus, emerging from the tomb.

He lay on the ground outside the steaming hole, gagging and gasping for oxygen. He observed the Caterpillar, as it stood like a war-weary relic, parts of it still glowing from the extreme heat of the fire. In the following days, his boss would chew him out for the damage done to this expensive piece of machinery. He had effectively disobeyed orders to stay out of harm's way, but he had also saved the neighborhood from utter destruction. At this moment, none of it mattered. He crawled up on his knees, lifted his head towards heaven, and mouthed a tearful "thank you" to the sky.

The following Sunday, Allen made his customary call to the pay phone in Gonzaga University's cafeteria, Kathie waiting expectantly on the other end.

"How was your week? How's Foss Lewis?" she asked. "I heard about the fires."

"That's what I wanted to talk to you about, Kathie… I started taking instructions for you… Now I want to be Catholic for me."

After Kathie and Allen hung up the phone that night, she spent the rest of it staring at her belongings, calculating as she often did about most things, just how long it might take her to put everything in her dorm room into a box.

Kathie Baranski decided that she had learned just about all she needed to at Gonzaga University. She had heard the words come out of his mouth for which she had prayed. All she knew was that she didn't want to waste another moment without Allen, and decided she knew enough about what it was going to take to start their life. The rest, as she puts it, would be solved by trusting God and working hard.

Allen hung up the phone that night and regarded his bloodstained, bandaged hand. From then on, Allen Lund's passion for pursuing the Catholic faith, and all for which it stood, unquenchably burned within him like wildfire.

* * *

"I picked him out from the beginning," Kathie said, reflecting on their early years together. She had a faraway look in her eyes and turned to gaze out of the windows of her house facing Johnston Lake. Reminiscing, she paused for a moment, lost in thought. Then with a glint in her eye, she said, "Well, he'd always say he picked me out." Kathie laughed, "If I hadn't picked him out, he wouldn't have gotten past 'hello.'" She explained, "There was no definitive moment. We just gradually got together. Maybe I wasn't as goofy as the other girls. He was attracted to me, I was attracted to him, it was meant to be."

It was convenient, but also effortless and natural. It wasn't love at first sight like the fairytales. However, for them, it was enough. Like everything else chronicled from that moment forward in the Lund family legacy, it was the only thing it needed to be: It was good.

CHAPTER FIVE

INSTRUCTIONS AND VOWS

"You will seek me, and you will find me when you seek me with all of your heart."

—*Jeremiah 29:13*

In all the fun escapades Allen and Ralph had together growing up, it should be noted that Allen didn't originally make it on the debate team. He wanted to try out to have more time to hang out with his friend, but his tryout didn't lead to success. However, Allen never was one to give up on things. He decided to start picking arguments with the teacher in charge of the team. Allen was in his class and he spent so much time debating him during class hours that eventually the teacher relented and officially put Allen on the team. The story is a glimpse at Allen's famous tenacity.

No one who ever put Allen Lund on their team ever regretted it, but it didn't mean that early on there wasn't a need for Allen to prove his value to his skeptics. Though Kathie was elated with Allen's decision to begin his instructions into the Catholic Church, some of the local clergy were more wary of the young man.

Father Kern, who had mentored Kathie in high school, did not take kindly to the young man vying for her heart. Before slamming the rectory door in Allen's face, Father Kern made it very clear he didn't trust Allen's intentions. He believed that Allen was only interested in the Catholic Church to win Kathie's heart. That may have been true at the outset, but Allen's motivations had changed. However, there was little Allen could say to convince the priest he was ready to take his own faith seriously, and taking faith seriously is something priests are known for doing.

Father Kern was adamant about cutting Allen out of Kathie Baranski's life. On one occasion after a youth group skiing trip, Father Kern, who chaperoned the trip Kathie was on, insisted on taking Kathie all the way home afterwards and dropping her off on her porch. He knew Allen was waiting for Kathie at the church parking lot, planning to pick her up and drive her home. However, Father Kern was determined to squash any of Allen's attempts at more time with Kathie.

It wasn't just Father Kern who provided opposition. Allen made an appointment to meet with Father Pollock, another local priest. When the time came for the meeting, Father Pollack never showed up. Opposition was fierce.

Allen was frustrated by the resistance he was getting from the local clergy. It was Kathie's friend June who stood up for Allen, speaking with Father Kern on Allen's behalf. She believed that Allen, despite not being Catholic, inherently possessed more of the fruits of the Spirit, and Christ-like characteristics than some people who had spent far more time adorning the church pews.

June loved how Allen loved Kathie. June also related to Allen a lot. They both grew up in similar economic situations and in one way or another had dealt with the pain of having a parent who struggled to fully embrace their responsibility as a parent. This gave June a greater compassion for her friend's fiance, so much so she agreed to be his sponsor. A sponsor in the Catholic Church is someone who agrees to support potential converts during their instructions. They provide consistent encouragement and prayer. June often joked that the hardest part of being Allen's sponsor was "holding him over the baptismal font." Truly, June could always make Allen laugh. Her lighthearted spirit uplifted him. Allen would need this support because any journey of discovery taken in earnest has its ups and downs.

Allen's instructions began while Kathie was still in Washington finishing up her semester at Gonzaga, which ended up being a blessing. Allen was forced to examine his motives for his quest towards God. He had many cosmic questions as he began to study, and in the process, he waded through every emotion from skepticism, to confusion, to awe. However, Allen remained humble and committed through it all.

There is a famous passage of scripture in Matthew nineteen where Jesus says, "Let the little children come to me, and do not hinder them, for it is those who are childlike that the Kingdom of Heaven belongs." In a sense, Allen did come to God like a child. Children don't understand everything, nor should they. They know enough to trust and obey. What Allen did know was that God had saved his life, looking after him that day in the fire. Allen also saw the genuine faith, joy, certainty, stability, and purpose God gave the woman he loved, so he wanted that, too. Following God seemed simply, "the right thing to do."

Allen began the study of God with authenticity, integrity, and curiosity. He was the type of guy who took apart appliances and everyday machines to figure out how they worked. This is the methodical way he tried to wrap his head around big theological concepts. When he struggled to understand or disagreed with something the Catholic Church said, he would confide in June.

Eventually, Father Vincent O'Sullivan, the Jesuit priest from St. Mary's Church in West Ogden, took Allen under his wing and conducted his Catholic formation lessons.

During his instructions, one of the hardest things for Allen to understand was the free gift of Grace. Perhaps more than any other trait or condition, Allen understood hard work. He had always earned everything he had, and the idea that Christ's

Grace was freely given rather than earned was a thought too wonderful to be understood, at least not at this point in Allen's life. However, serving God by loving people was just the sort of practical idea Allen could readily absorb. It was also that simple faith walked out that turned Allen into the great philanthropist he came to be.

Allen's faith shaped the entire trajectory of his life, and his understanding of God rapidly evolved from the summer of 1958 through the spring of 1960. He first viewed God as a mystery, unsure if there was someone up there watching over him. Then God was an obstacle, a mountain he must climb to marry the woman he loved. Then God was his savior, worthy of being followed. Then He was a boss, the most worthwhile Person to commit your life to serving.

With the guidance of Father O'Sullivan and the help of his godmother, June, Allen Lund was baptized on May 24, 1960 into the Roman Catholic Church.

Years later Allen would make the final transition and learn to receive God as his Father. This kind of Love took longer to accept since Allen's relationship with his biological father was strained at best, but that Love had already gripped Allen, whether he realized it or not, and it became the thing that fortified his life.

* * *

"Hey, Arf?" Allen beckoned a stoic Ralph under his breath. Ralph stood rigidly at the front of the church, the perfect picture of a dutiful best man. They were thirty minutes into the wedding ceremony, a day Allen and Kathie had looked forward to with great anticipation. Back then Catholic masses were still conducted in Latin. Allen called to his friend again trying to quietly get his attention, "Arf?"

"What?" Ralph awkwardly whispered back. "What are you doing?"

"Tell me something," Allen murmured.

"What? Turn around." Ralph responded nervously.

"I've got no idea what they're sayin' up there. Am I married yet or what?" Allen asked with a wink. The friends had to choke back laughter for the rest of the ceremony.

Kathie and Allen were married on Saturday, July 16, 1960 at St. Joseph's Catholic Church in Ogden UT. It was a small wedding with close friends and family. June and Ralph served as Maid of Honor and Best Man. Kathie's young step sisters—Jeanie, Theresa, and Michelle—were the little flower girls. Kathie's dress was made for her by Edith, her stepfather's mother. A skilled seamstress, she wanted Kathie to feel extra special on this happy day. Kathie's stepfather worked hard to fix up the backyard and garage of their home, which would serve as the site of the wedding reception. It was a small wedding, not a lot of fuss, but as Kathie reflected on it years later, she said, "It was perfect!"

CHAPTER SIX
A LUNDERFUL LIFE

"If you want to change the world, go home and love your family."
—*Mother Teresa*

In the Book of Genesis, the story of creation includes the earliest written description of marriage. The woman, Eve, is created from the rib of the man, Adam, and becomes a helpmate suitable for him. This institution was created and ordained by God, and of it, God says, "For this reason, a man leaves his father and mother and is united with his wife, and they shall become one flesh."

The challenge of merging two lives into one isn't easy, no matter how much love people share between them. Kathie and Allen had two very different personalities, and melding their lives together would mean huge adjustments. The happy couple went to Jackson Hole, Wyoming for their honeymoon. The honeymoon was only for one night because Allen needed to return to work at Foss Lewis the next day. Allen was industrious, energetic, and had an unparalleled work ethic, but budgeting and balancing a checkbook weren't things he ever previously thought about. As a single man, if he had the money for something he bought it. If someone was in need and Allen had money to give, he gave it. However, now that he had a wife to support and bills to pay, the need for financial organization became very important.

The couple pinched pennies to buy their first home from Allen's maternal grandfather. They paid him five hundred dollars above the listed price. The house was a two-bedroom with a full basement equipped with a washing machine and subterranean drain. It wasn't grand, and the home needed work, but Allen was a motivated buyer. He and Kathie were expecting their first child in June of 1961.

Allen's financial mindset was to continue to create revenue that could eventually outrun the bills. He was cavalier about money, and this made Kathie extremely nervous. She loved Allen's jovial, carefree nature, but worried how it may factor into his ability to provide stability.

"Where did this bill come from?" Kathie asked, finding the crumpled envelope in one of Allen's pants pockets before tossing the clothing into the laundry hamper.

"Oh, I forgot about that. I was going to pay it," Allen replied calmly.

"When? With what?" Kathie asked.

"Look, it will work out. I just hadn't gotten around to it." Allen retorted.

"Well, Mr. Lund, it's a very good thing that you married me," she shot back with a smile, diffusing the tension.

Allen was indeed lucky to have Kathie. Her analytic mind and experience as a cashier at Lagoon came in handy. She was meticulous and detail-oriented, and took over the family bookkeeping. In a sense, these two very distinct personalities became the perfect balance for each other. They were opposites, but each had strengths that offset the other's weaknesses.

The common thread binding Allen and Kathie was their faith-filled commitment to helping others. They didn't have much at this stage of life. However, what they did have, they shared with those in need, even when it wasn't easy. They were known for this generosity later in life as they supported countless philanthropic organizations, but their spirit of giving had nothing to do with money and excess.

That enduring commitment to the well-being of others was exemplified when Ralph transferred to Brigham Young University to finish his accounting degree. He then headed for the LDS Great Lakes Mission for two years. He recalled that Allen and Kathie were dirt poor, living in that clapboard house while Allen wrestled Caterpillars all day for Foss Lewis. Ralph was concerned for his best friend, wondering if he and Kathie had indeed gotten married too young, especially because Allen would confide in Ralph that the body-breaking work was not the type of thing he could sustain for much longer. Then one day, Ralph received an envelope in the mail. A fifty-dollar-check arrived from Allen and Kathie designated as support for Ralph's mission. "What most people don't understand about Allen was that he had been generous his whole life. So he didn't wait till he made a lot of money to be generous. He always was, he was just pure in heart." Ralph reflected years later.

From September 1960 to September 1962, Allen and Kathie would frequently send fifty dollar donations to Ralph to support his LDS mission. It didn't matter that they were Catholic and Ralph was Mormon. They simply wanted to support their friend. Allen was still wet behind the ears as far as Catholic converts go, but he never lost the freshness of wanting to simply help the people he loved. Allen had a love greater than legalism. It was this simplicity of demonstrated faith that would allow him to transcend political, philosophical, and denominational divides to accomplish great feats in industry and philanthropy throughout his life.

This was who the Lunds were, even in the earliest stages of their shared journey. If there was ever a door-to-door salesman or Girl Scout in the neighborhood, they were lucky to knock on Allen's door. He wanted to support people, and although he insisted on hearing the entire sales pitch and asked countless follow-up questions, there was no doubt that if he was able, he was going to buy whatever they were selling.

Loving others wasn't always easy. It required sacrifice to share what they had. A few weeks after their wedding Kathie and Allen took Allen's father into their home. Wayne and Maxine had divorced and he had fallen into a tough financial time. It was difficult for Kathie, a newly married woman, to have her father-in-law sleeping on her couch. Yet she was every match for Allen in the depth of her compassion. Wayne overstayed his welcome, often charming and manipulating Allen into allowing him to stick around. This probably would've gone on even longer than it did, but with children on the way Allen's protective instincts eventually pushed him to show his father some tough love. He stayed till he got back on his feet, but Allen set a hard timeline on the generosity.

Allen had a strained relationship with Wayne, but he never spoke an ill word about his father to anyone. Allen wasn't the type to judge a man battling inner demons. He loved Wayne and supported and prayed for him. Wayne never did overcome his drinking habit and eventually died of alcohol-related liver cancer. It was Allen who supported him in his old age, taking care of him as if the parenting roles were reversed.

Allen knew that he would be the father to his children that his own father never was to him. He didn't want his family to struggle financially, and he was determined to be a constant presence in his children's lives. Their first child, David Lund, was born on June 18, 1961. The Lunds were in a parish with many young couples with children, so David was an exciting new addition to the community. It wasn't long after David's arrival that Allen and Kathie spent $16,500 to build their second house. At the intersection of skill and necessity, Allen dug the basement himself.

Their family rapidly expanded. Kathie was twenty-one years old when Natalie, their second child, came in December of 1962. Following her were Kenny, Eddie, and Anna; and years later when the family moved to California, Christina.

Adjusting to parenthood proved just as challenging as the adjustments to married life. There were more mouths to feed and the house reeled from the specific kind of chaos only young siblings born close together can create. Allen was a natural calming force in the home, but he worked all day leaving Kathie on the front lines from morning until evening. The young father got in the habit of hanging out with coworkers after work. In a time before cell phones, this would leave Kathie clueless about her husband's whereabouts.

"Where have you been?" Kathie asked after Allen walked in the door.

"What do you mean?" he asked.

Kathie explained nervously, "Foss Lewis called several times wanting to talk to you. Are you alright?"

"I'm fine, Kathie, I'm here," Allen said. He kissed her on the cheek and walked into the kitchen.

"Well, I was worried," she said following after him.

"Don't worry about me," Allen said. He had gotten off work at four o'clock but had not walked through his front door until seven-thirty. Kathie decided not to press the issue any further. She struggled with not being able to get a hold of Allen, and she also struggled to express just how much she needed him to be home as soon as possible after work. She'd spent the whole day wrangling children and was desperate for a break herself.

Kathie didn't have a confrontational personality, but she knew how to get her husband to understand her point of view without having to use words. Kathie and Allen would take turns going to Mass on the weekends. Allen would attend the eight o'clock service while Kathie watched the kids at home, and then Allen would watch the children while Kathie went to the ten o'clock Mass. One week when Allen was staying home with the kids, Kathie didn't rush home after church. She stayed out most of the day finding places to hide around town.

When she finally did get home, Allen was in the thick of some exuberant chaos with the children. When he finally caught Kathie's eye, the two just stared at each other for a moment, before Allen cracked an all-knowing smile. He laughed and shook his head, finally appreciating how hard Kathie worked with the kids every day. After that, Allen was rarely home late from work and if he was Kathie never bothered him again about his whereabouts. The two trusted and supported each other.

The couple fell into a healthy swing as parents, sharing duties and communicating in their own unique ways. Life was busy, messy, and beautiful. Yet, despite his loving wife, his healthy children, and their wonderful community, Allen struggled with a burning inside of him, a lone ember that existed since the fire. He felt strongly that God had a purpose for his life that went beyond just living his own version of happily ever after. God had saved him from the burning bushfire in the Wasatch mountains, and Allen wanted to live a life worthy of the second chance he was given; that calling he had received.

CHAPTER SEVEN

BOUNTIFUL BLESSINGS

"In friendship, we think we have chosen our peers…but for the Christian, there are, strictly speaking, no chances. A secret master of ceremonies has been at work."

—*CS Lewis*

Scripture teaches that the steps of a righteous person are ordered by the Lord. This was certainly always true for Kathie Lund, whose faithful prayers always seemed to be answered in unexpected ways through the ordinary people she brought lovingly into her circle of friends. Allen benefitted from the prayers of his loving wife, as all men who choose great life partners do. Looking through the rear-view mirror at the Lunds' journey, it's easy to see divine providence plotting the course that led Allen Lund to accomplish all he did in his lifetime. However, at the time of their occurrence, those divine appointments seemed ordinary and inconsequential.

Allen and Kathie felt very blessed to be living in Bountiful,

Utah. There was a strong Catholic community there, and the young families helped create a thriving ecosystem of support at St. Olaf's Parish. Each month the parish hosted events and parties in the church hall. The environment provided Allen the opportunity to grow deeper in his faith because he had a plethora of male mentors surrounding him. Kathie also thrived with the support as a young mom. The community gave her places to take the kids and friends who understood the ins and outs of motherhood. It was a game changer.

"Well, it's lovely to meet you, Kathie Lund," Mary Lowe said. She was a fellow parishioner at St. Olaf's. "We've decided, if we have a girl, to name this one 'Kathy,' I'm not sure if you spell it with a 'y' too," Mary said while rubbing her very pregnant stomach.

"'I-e,'" Kathie responded.

"There you go," Mary laughed. "Well, we moms will have to stick together."

Kathie was also visibly pregnant with their third child at this time. She was excited to meet another young mother in the same stage of life as her, especially one who shared her faith and devotion to the church. The two women met through the Altar Society, an organization of parishioners—predominantly women—who maintain the sanctuary and ceremonial items used in worship.

"So how long have you been coming to the Altar Society meetings?" Mary asked.

"Tonight is my first night. I thought it was lovely," Kathie responded excitedly.

"It always is. I love it because I get to be around more women of faith, but if you want to have some real fun, you need to join the League."

"The League?" Kathie asked.

"Oh yes, the League of Women Voters. We meet up each week to learn about water, the city, heck, the whole country and environment. At least that's what I tell my husband, Roger."

"I see." Kathie said, confused.

Mary took Kathie in for a moment, cracked a smile and leaned in. "Listen, that man and I have two children under the age of two at home and another on the way. The League really allows me another excuse to have an hour or two outside the house each week."

Kathie smiled at Mary, recognizing in her a kindred spirit.

"I know what you mean. This baby will be our third. My husband Allen and I have a son, David, and a daughter, Natalie. So I know how hectic a house with small children can be. I even joined a bowling team because the alley that I go to has childcare. It gives me a few hours. The fringe benefit is I've actually gotten pretty good at bowling, too." Kathie explained.

The two women laughed together, and in that moment

became instant friends. They naturally assumed their husbands would hit it off as well. They decided to bring their families together at the next church function. A few days later, Allen Lund and Roger Lowe were introduced to one another at the St. Olaf's family picnic. Allen tried to make small talk by asking Roger what he did for a living, but Roger was too distracted by the cuts, burns, and bandages on Allen's body, his merit badges from another week of being tossed around by Foss Lewis' heavy machinery. Roger's reserved responses only provoked Allen's natural curiosity. Roger worked for a company called C.H. Robinson. The company bought and sold produce and moved it all over the country using big rig trucks. Allen didn't know anything about the produce distribution industry and had a million questions for Roger, who was tired from a full week of work. After a few awkward exchanges, and strained conversation, the men stopped conversing altogether.

The indifferent reviews these two men had of each other didn't deter Kathie and Mary, who were still determined they should be friends. Roger was taking their son on his first fishing trip up in the mountains that week, and the women decided to plan another opportunity for their husbands to get together when Roger returned. They hoped their husbands would be open-minded to the idea.

* * *

WHAM! Roger's station wagon came to a halt while crossing a mountain stream on the way to what was supposed to be a promising fishing spot. Roger had been wanting to take his son on a father-son fishing trip for a while, and he had finally carved out space in the schedule to make it happen.

"Tommy, stay right here, buddy," Roger said to his wide-eyed two year old sitting perplexed in the backseat. The sudden stop had jarred them both. The country road crossed several creeks on the way up the mountain and the vehicle was lodged on something in the stream. The impact had locked up the transmission gears, so Roger couldn't back up onto the road. He got out to investigate. Carefully maneuvering in a foot of icy cold mountain water around the AMC Rambler, Roger tried not to slip.

Unable to see any exterior damage to the Rambler, Roger got down on his hands and knees for a look. That's when he saw the issue: a large rock was wedged between the ground and driveshaft. Roger shook his head in disbelief. He stood up, opened the driver door, and climbed back into the car.

"Where did you go, Daddy?" Tommy asked.

"Hold on buddy." Roger began fiddling with the gear shift to no avail. It was no use; the gears were seized. Roger grabbed a piece of paper out of his coat pocket and unfolded it. It was a hand drawn map with words inscribed on it: "Hey Roger! This is the spot! You and Tommy will love it there! Have fun. Love, Charlie."

Roger studied the map for a few moments. Finally he muttered under his breath, "Well thanks a lot for the tip, Charlie… you're fired."

With Tommy on his shoulders, Roger marched through the rugged terrain until they were able to hitch a ride to the nearest town: Morgan, Utah. Roger reached into his wallet and pulled out a few bucks to hand to the camper who provided the ride, but the man refused. He explained that the nearest tow truck was a hundred miles away so Roger should save his money.

From a pay phone at a general store in Roger called Mary at their house back in Bountiful, explaining everything that happened and asking her to send help. When Mary and Roger hung up the phone she immediately dialed Kathie Lund.

"Hey Kathie," Mary said, "I need a favor and also… I think I got it figured out."

* * *

Roger paced around the store. It had been hours since he saw anyone other than the store clerk, let alone another vehicle on the road. He was running out of ways to entertain his two year old son. After a few hours a pickup truck rolled into the parking lot of the general store. The pickup door swung open, and out stepped a mountain of a man: Allen Lund.

Allen was perhaps the last person Roger would have wanted to show up for him that day. He judged Allen at their first meeting, and didn't give him a glowing review when Mary later pressed him for an opinion. Allen's presence was like another slice of the day-long humble pie for Roger. Allen pulled Roger's car out of the stream that day and got them back on the road. In typical Allen Lund fashion, he didn't make a big deal out of the episode. He was just helping another person. But before they parted ways and started the journey home, Allen's curiosity peaked again.

"Roger, let me ask you something," he said.

"Uh, Yes?" Roger muttered wearily.

"Did you really bring a passenger car onto this road?" Allen held back a smile.

Rogers' shoulders sank. The day had worn him down. Allen put his bandaged hand on Roger's shoulder. With a sheepish grin he said, "You know, Rodge, I've done some pretty stupid things in my day, too."

There was something in the way Allen said it, because Roger immediately burst out in laughter. Allen, who seemed to have been holding back a chuckle the whole time, joined in. The two men finally had a moment of recognition of each other, and like their wives, bonded over that laugh.

"C'mon, Roger," Allen said, "I think the ladies have some dinner for us at home."

Allen and Roger were friends from that day forward.

Even though the Lowes and the Lunds lived on opposite

sides of Bountiful, the two families became the best of friends, just as Mary and Kathie had schemed. Both families had four children at the time, and because they were all born close together, the kids became playmates. It was nice for Kathie and Mary, being often pregnant at the same time, to talk with each other about motherhood and life. The friendship made this season one that they all remembered fondly. The couples would take turns babysitting all the kids so the other couple could attend Mass that week. They also hosted each other for dinners and poker nights. There was not a lot of money then, so instead of beer they drank Dr. Pepper. The parties would go late into the evening and it was a good chance to wear the kids out so they'd go to sleep easier.

The families grew increasingly close and comfortable in beautiful Bountiful. It seemed that they would go on like that for the rest of their lives. Financially they didn't have much between them, but they had each other and that seemed to always be enough.

However, divine providence would have it that this friendship would shift Allen Lund's life forever in a way he never would have expected.

CHAPTER EIGHT

OATMEAL

"You have stayed long enough at this mountain, break camp and advance."

—*Deuteronomy 1:6-7*

Every winter when the snow began, the workload for Foss Lewis would dwindle. To keep busy earning their hours, Allen and other members of the crew would take time to repair old equipment. Allen always took initiative, but there was less and less work to do to stay employed and his hours had already been cut drastically. Many employees had been laid off and Allen was suddenly insecure about working for a tight knit family company considering he was one of the only remaining employees who wasn't a son or a son-in-law. Winter wasn't kind to the wallet or the wallet bearer. The vehicle cabins were not heated, leaving Allen's body aching from every bump and jar of the freezing work days. It was a difficult season, but he had Kathie at home sustaining his optimism.

"Allen, I know the job is wearing on you, but it's all we have right now," Kathie consoled her husband.

"It would be different if there was any overtime, but I'm running out of things to do," Allen lamented.

Kathie mustered, "I ran the numbers. Even if they cut you back an additional 10 percent, we will have enough to make it until the spring."

"Kathie, I'm tired of just making it." Allen confessed, "I don't know how much longer we can keep this up."

Kathie's eyes widened as Allen rolled up his sleeve, exposing another machine induced wound. "I don't mind the work or a bruise here or there, for you and the kids, but if something ever really happens to me…well I may not be dead, but Kathie, being home injured, with hungry kids, that's not living either."

"What do you think we should do?" Kathie worried aloud.

"I don't know," he said, observing her. "I just can't keep doing this for a business we won't ever have a piece of."

He gave her a reassuring smile before walking away and swinging open the door to the kid's bedroom. She listened as the boisterous sounds of the little ones' excitement echoed down the hall. Daddy was home. They giggled as Allen let out a bear growl and proceeded to chase them around the room. Something resembling Wrestle Mania ensued as the kids tackled their dad. Kathie stood down the hall frozen with heavy thoughts. She had married a good man; a man who always showed up for his family. He was hard working, consistent, and present. He shouldered the burdens of life and uncertainty, doing his best to shield his family from concern. Kathie approached the door frame, peeking her head inside the children's room. She gazed at the bravest man she'd ever seen.

Allen knew the probability of getting laid off was very high, so to mitigate the income deficit winter brought on and give his family some financial cushion, Allen started working nights. He got involved with the local chapter of the Knights of Columbus, selling insurance. The Knights of Columbus is a global Catholic fraternal service organization. They participate in a variety of charitable activities, but also consist of a wholly-owned insurance company that focuses on providing coverage to working class and migrant families. Allen was always a people person, no matter what social setting or business endeavor. He enjoyed working for the Knights and would buy beer for the members of the chapter. What Allen did naturally out of his love for people, ended up organically expanding his network.

Beer nights became so popular among the Knights of Columbus and the community as a whole, that Allen decided to have several pallets of Fischer beer delivered to his house. The beer was cheap and the taste reflected it, but it endeared Allen to the community. He had an outdoor carport and would keep the beer there unguarded, though no one ever bothered it. Other members of the Knights would even come and buy beer off Allen, but he sold the beer at cost because Allen wasn't interested in making a profit from this. It was simply something fun to do for his colleagues and neighbors. Beer wasn't his commodity; creating and maintaining deep relationships was. This was an intrinsic quality that made Allen Lund a success in everything he put his hand to. That year the Knights of Columbus made Allen Lund Knight of the Year.

Eventually work at Foss Lewis became so slow that Allen was laid off and his second job with the Knights wasn't enough to cover costs. Allen had no choice but to go on unemployment. The family couldn't possibly tighten the belt anymore than they already had. Kathie and Allen discussed options. He would try to expand his insurance selling side-hustle, but it was a slow build, not immediately financially fruitful, and not work he enjoyed as a long-term solution. They discussed the possibility of Kathie taking a job outside of the home, but it was difficult with little ones. What they really needed was a breakthrough, an answer to their prayers for financial provision that could carry the family forward. They prayed together and Kathie also asked their friends Mary and Roger to pray for them.

Days later, a 50-pound bag of oatmeal mysteriously showed up on the Lund doorstep. No one knew who it was from. It wasn't from Mary and Roger, and no note was left with the surprise gift. Kathie speculates one of their Mormon neighbors, who owned a bakery in town, could have delivered it to them at night.

However, to this day no one has claimed credit. Regardless, the Lund children ate the oatmeal for months, though to them it felt like years. It was a challenge for Kathie to figure out as many ways as possible to cook the oats. She tried various presentations. She baked it into loafs, fried it into patties, and scooped it out as porridge, stretching the bag for as far as it could go.

That simple act of kindness was an answer to their prayers and it sustained the family. It didn't just fill up Kathie's plate. It filled up her faith that God did in fact hear her prayers and that He cared deeply about what her family was going through. The family got through the winter and spring living on oatmeal, the deer Allen would hunt, canned preserves, and the apricots from the three trees in their yard that bloomed early that year. It was gratitude for these humble provisions that made this season a special one for the Lund family. As a catskinner who leveled land, Allen knew that when life brings you down to the bottom, it's to make sure you have the right foundation. Kathie and Allen built their foundation on reliance on God and love for each other. They would build up their life from there.

* * *

In 1967, Roger had hired a new associate to work at his branch of CH Robinson, a produce wholesaler. However, his new hire was an immediate disappointment. The applicant looked great on paper, but couldn't broker a deal to save his life. His presentation came off as flashy and untrustworthy and he couldn't close a sale. Roger needed to find a replacement and fast. Business was booming and he needed help to keep up. He wanted someone who was good with people.

"What about Allen?" Mary, his wife, offered.

"Allen?" Roger said in a tone of surprise.

"Of course! You know he's great with people!" Mary added enthusiastically.

"I know, but they're our friends. What if he doesn't work out? You think I'm going to be able to fire him, knowing he's got another baby on the way?" Roger objected.

Mary just stared at her perspiring husband, rubbing her own very pregnant stomach. She and Kathie were once again pregnant and due near the same time of year. Mary knew the stress their household would be under if Roger could not find a good assistant. They were headed into watermelon season, their busiest time of year. She convinced Roger to at least approach Allen with the opportunity. He was hesitant because of their friendship. He didn't want to cross personal and professional lines and he couldn't picture the big machine guy sitting behind a desk making calls.

Nevertheless, he approached Allen with the job and let Allen know about his reservations. After listening to Roger, Allen convinced his friend to give him a shot. Allen needed a job and Roger needed the help. It seemed simple enough to Allen, and he reassured his friend that it would work out. Allen had confidence in his ability to pick things up and do things well. He recognized that his friend felt he was taking a chance on him, but he knew he wouldn't let a friend down.

So Allen was hired and trained on the telephones. Unfortunately, right around the same time, Roger's sixty-nine-year-old father died following a severe stroke, forcing Roger to leave Allen alone while he left for Iowa to attend the funeral. In an instant, the man he had reservations about even training was about to run his entire brokerage office.

Whether it was change being flung from patron pockets on the Lagoon roller coaster, or dirt being moved with an excavator, Allen understood intuitively how to make money moving things on a machine from one place to another. He had grown up around big machinery and the men who operated them. He understood the challenges and point of view of the truckers shipping the produce, but his time selling insurance had also taught him how to present and close a deal with the guys sitting in their offices. Allen instantly became a wonderful communicator and broker.

On Allen's first day on the job without Roger, there were trucks on the road needing to be dispatched. Allen got on the telephone, negotiated the loads for four trucks, and nearly doubled the average day's revenue. He dispelled all of Roger's concerns about whether he would be a good fit in the industry.

One of Roger's clients, the Butry Food Chain out of Montana, not only booked their regular loads, but booked others because of Allen. Roger breathed a sigh of relief when he returned. Suddenly, he knew he had found more than a suitable assistant. Roger sensed Allen was destined for greatness in the produce brokering business. From then on, their work together grew more and more successful, and the personal relationship deepened as well. At last, the prayers of Kathie and Mary were answered, and it appeared that they and their children would spend the rest of their lives in Bountiful as the best of friends.

Roger referred to the three days Allen was alone at his office at C.H. Robinson as "baptism by fire," yet marveled at how successful he was. It wasn't until later that Roger discovered that part of his extraordinary confidence was due in part to the fact that Allen Lund had been baptized by fire before.

Roger quickly realized there was something different about Allen Lund. His work ethic was unparalleled. He was at work every day at 4:00 a.m. to meet with the guys selling produce. He was an excellent negotiator and his authenticity and genuine love for the job attracted people to him. He also knew how to talk to truckers because he understood their jobs from working with his father at a young age. This made him excellent at lining up transportation for the produce he needed to get to his customers. He organized his day strategically, moving perishable produce in the early morning and dry commodities like cotton in the early afternoon.

Allen soon figured out he could broker more than just produce. His customers needed trucks assigned to transport the purchased produce to their locations. Allen saw an opportunity. He would line up transportation for his clients, pay the truckers, and then charge his clients a commission for brokering their transportation. Allen's relationships with the truckers made this an organic addition to the work he was already doing. He was excellent at organizing the logistics, and the additional commisions started to make that branch of C.H. Robinson a lot more money.

When Allen started brokering, he was shipping cotton, peanuts, and produce from Los Angeles to Houston. C.H. Robinson had shippers all over the United States, and Allen was in a prime location to make a widespread impact.

Word soon got back to the corporate headquarters of C.H. Robinson in Minneapolis about Allen's accomplishments. At the time, C.H. Robinson was only a produce brokerage company. Representatives from their corporate office made special trips to meet with and interview Allen. When asked how he became so successful so quickly, Allen simply remarked, "Roger taught me everything I know."

After working for Roger for three years, the leadership at C.H. Robinson decided it was time for Allen to replicate elsewhere the model he had built in Utah. They called Roger and told him they were sending Allen to their office at the produce market in downtown Los Angeles to broker and develop a similar logistics system, noting the L.A. market was larger and blossoming with opportunities. The news didn't surprise Roger. He had watched Allen's successful growth, but he was sad to lose his close proximity with such a good friend. The Lunds had also just delivered their fifth child. Adorable Anna Lund was only three months old, the Lund household was busier than ever, and Roger regretted the timing of the news he had to deliver to Allen. However, the corporate office made it clear: they wanted Allen Lund on a plane to Los Angeles as soon as possible.

Roger and Mary would miss their friends, the nights playing cards, and getting all of the children together. Yet Roger knew Allen's future was bigger than Bountiful. The couple cherished the remaining time they had with them in town. They attended the big farewell party Allen's mother, Maxine, threw for them. Family and friends who attended, filled two suitcases with men and womens clothing. The party attendees dressed in attire opposite of their gender for laughs. They played games outdoors in their funny homemade costumes. Laughter is what everyone needed because they were sad to see Allen and his family go.

In 1969, Allen and Kathie Lund packed up their children—David (eight), Natalie (seven), Kenny (four), Eddie (two), and nine-month-old Anna—and moved from Bountiful, Utah to

Los Angeles, California. All Roger and Mary felt was that they were losing a part of themselves, and both shed tears as they helplessly watched their best friends drive away.

Even after the move, Allen would call Roger nearly every day, asking for continued advice and mentorship. Allen was a forward thinker. He knew God was handing him an opportunity to improve life for himself and his family. So he put his foot to the gas and didn't look back. He didn't let off the gas personally and he wouldn't professionally, either. He knew that incredible opportunities were ahead and he was ready for them.

CHAPTER NINE

YE THOUGH I WALK THROUGH DEATH VALLEY

"It's one thing to have talent. It's another to figure out how to use it."
—*Roger Miller*

Allen and Kathie packed up their Valiant station wagon with their five young children, dog, and semi-sedated cat who didn't appreciate the trip one bit. It was a crowded and eventful journey, to put it mildly. The drive to Los Angeles was long, with everyone crammed together. The trip included crossing the desert of Death Valley, one of the hottest geographical regions on Earth, in the middle of summer. Running the air conditioning was out of the question, because the car engine was in danger of overheating. Kathie had a bottle of ice water to dampen napkins to place on the kids foreheads and necks to battle the intense heat. Still, Allen and Kathie played games with the children to keep up morale. Often on road trips, Allen would have the children compete to see who could spot notable landmarks first. He also had them try to guess the exact time of their arrival. The person who guessed closest to the minute won the game.

No one remembers who won that particular game, only that all of their guesses were thrown off on the I-5 when the family excitedly passed the moving van carrying all of their furniture and belongings. All of them waved at the driver as they flew past them, and in the excitement Allen missed his exit to the 134 E. The kids watched the van drive in the right direction towards Glendale CA, realizing the missed turn just added more time to what was already a long trip.

Allen had selected Glendale because it was where several of his new co-workers lived with their families. Allen felt it was important to live near the people with whom he would work. They didn't know anyone in Los Angeles yet, and that was their best chance at forming a good community for the kids. He also knew how important getting involved in a church would be for his family, so he selected a house on Isabel Street near Incarnation Church.

Arriving in town was exciting for everyone. The kids were in awe of the old eight story Crocker Bank building in Glendale. It was the tallest building the children had ever seen. They felt they had finally arrived in "the big city."

There would be many transitions to come. Glendale was a crowded suburbia of cookie cutter neighborhood streets set up in a grid. The yards were smaller and the houses a lot closer together than the family had grown accustomed to in Utah. However, amid all of the changes, the Lunds quickly took to the neighborhood. The older kids were sent to play outside and instructed to come home when the street lamps came on in the evening.

The neighborhood was full of young families with children, so the Lund kids quickly connected with friends along their street. They also got settled right away into church which made the transition easier for them. Soon school would start again and the Lund children would be fully adjusted to life in the new city. Since Allen was expected to start work almost immediately upon their arrival, the kids' smooth transition was a blessing to Kathie, who was saddled with the bulk of unpacking and took on the responsibility of turning a house into a home.

Allen loved working for CH Robinson. He loved it so much that he felt he would one day retire with the company. The Los Angeles produce market was an exciting new adventure for him. The market opened at 3:00 a.m. and ran till noon, and there Allen was in his element among the hustle and bustle of it all, with noisy trucks and boisterous voices shouting to close deals. Allen got up each day at 4:00 a.m. to walk through the market during its exhilarating peak periods. Allen meandered through the market as if he was its mayor. He learned and remembered everyone's name who worked there; and he knew about their lives and their families. He didn't just create connections; he made friends. He would also buy cases of fruits and vegetables and anything else he found at a good price and bring them home to Kathie. Everything they got, they got in bulk. It wasn't until the kids were older that they realized fruit wasn't always bought by the crate. Years later, the children marveled that someone could go into a supermarket and buy just one apple.

Allen loved to work, and for him there was something inherently satisfying about coordinating loads and trucks. Though he initially began work with the dual approach he started in Utah, which was brokering produce in the morning and trucks by the afternoon, the transportation logistics part of his job became more and more important to him. It was important to CH Robinson's corporate office, as well. That was the very reason they had brought Allen Lund to Los Angeles.

In the early stages of any change in a company, it's difficult for everyone to understand the opportunities that lie in the shifts that are happening. The leadership in the Los Angeles branch of CH Robinson didn't think what Allen was doing was particularly difficult or useful. They were, at that time, primarily a produce brokerage company and Allen's work didn't seem central to their core mission. Allen's strength lay in his ability to see the big picture, so he maintained his belief in the opportunities transportation brokerage had to offer. Leadership didn't realize it at the time, but Allen was helping to build a brand new branch of revenue for them, forming a new company structure which would one day become their primary company model.

Like a crab outgrows its shell, or a child outgrows their clothes, Allen would constantly outgrow any container into which he was placed. This time the container was produce. Allen coordinated trucks for all the produce business CH Robinson had on the west coast, but he saw that there was more time in the day to broker other commodities beyond the produce market. He started to form new relationships and recruited new non-produce customers to CH Robinson.

Allen's efforts were generating revenue for CH Robinson of more than one hundred thousand dollars each year, but his paycheck wasn't reflecting his contribution. Allen had to fight for every raise he earned. They were reluctantly given over. As in his other business dealings, Allen was strategic in his relationship with CH Robinson management. Before he moved to Los Angeles, he had asked for a modest raise. In Roger's office there was a foot pedal connected to the phone system that could mute the speaker on their end and still allow Roger and Allen to hear their customers on the calls. On the other end of the call it sounded to the customer like they had been placed on a brief hold. This mute pedal was a helpful tool in a busy office. When leadership at CH Robinson called to discuss Allen's compensation in Los Angeles, Allen decided he wanted to get a better sense of what they were going to offer. After some time deliberating on the phone with them, Allen asked to place them on a hold. He pushed down the foot pedal and overheard their conversation.

"We're not paying him a penny more than one thousand dollars a month," they said.

Listening, Allen released the pedal, came back onto the call and said, "Listen guys, I just don't know if I'll be able to make this change happen for less than one thousand dollars a month."

Those initial negotiations set his rate, and despite his innovation and years of consistent work ethic, he was still only making fourteen thousand dollars a year. He and Kathie had five children. It was a busy home with a lot of mouths to feed, and the couple were making many sacrifices to continue their children's private education. Kathie made the decision to take a job moonlighting at a machine shop that did injection molding to form various plastic parts. She worked from 10:00 p.m. until 6:00 a.m. with a short break at 2:00 a.m. She would come home in time to get the kids off to school and take a short nap before the youngest kids got going for the day. This helped them make ends meet, but the idea of his wife, a mother of five children, working the night shift didn't sit well with Allen.

Once again he felt the familiar pain he had experienced while working for Foss Lewis. He worked so hard at his job, but ultimately for a company he would never have a piece of, and this wasn't sustainable for his family. Profit sharing was supposed to be a part of Allen's compensation package, but he wasn't seeing the fruits of his labor. In addition to believing his pay did not reflect his value, he also had some issues with the company culture at the Los Angeles office. He didn't like the attitude other brokers had towards truckers, with whom Allen felt a cherished kinship. He didn't like unprofessional language and yelling on the phone. Allen even installed a thicker door to his office, which he intentionally selected far down the hall from his colleagues. This was to insulate him from the way other people were doing business in the office. He wanted to do business his way, and began to imagine what it would be like to strike out on his own.

Allen worked at the LA office of CH Robinson from 1969 to 1976. He got along with his colleagues, but he was in a different life stage than many of them. The brokers would often go for a drink together after a long day at work. Allen, in contrast, headed straight home to help Kathie with the kids. Christina Lund, their sixth and youngest child, had just been born and was still under a year old. Watching the kids, juggling their activities, and getting dinner on the table required the same logistical genius he utilized at work.

When setting out on a new venture, a wise person considers their motives. When their reason for doing something is strong enough, they will figure out any means necessary to accomplish what they set out to do. Allen looked at his kids around the dinner table. They were his reason. He wanted to feed his family and give them a good life; not just scrape by. Watching them was like fodder to the early sparks that would lead to the formation of the Allen Lund Company. However, leaving his job was risky.

He needed to talk to Kathie. She listened intently to her husband explain his dream of building a new company. He would focus solely on transportation brokerage and be able to expand that industry. He would be able to conduct business on his own terms. He would establish a new company culture where truckers were considered customers just as much as the shippers were. He felt he could take care of all his clients and take care of the truckers, giving them a greater sense of importance and dignity.

The couple had a long discussion about this plan. Kathie listened intently as Allen explained his thought process. There would be difficulties and future challenges. Allen had weighed the pros and cons. The risk was very real, but ultimately Kathie trusted her husband and supported him. She believed wholeheartedly Allen would be successful. He had a natural logic, powerful mind, and formidable memory. Ultimately, Allen Lund had great gut instincts and over the years Kathie learned she could rely on them.

To bet on oneself and what you're able to do with God's help is brave when the stakes are so high. Allen had six young children at home and one thousand dollars in the bank, so the stakes couldn't have been higher for him to succeed. After some prayer and Kathie's blessing, Allen planned his next moves.

CHAPTER TEN
PIGGY BANKS

"If he fails, at least he fails while daring greatly, so that his place shall never be with those cold and timid souls who neither know victory nor defeat."

—*President Theodore Roosevelt,*
"The Man in the Arena"

Growing up in Utah, Allen Lund learned to hunt with his father. When starting a family of his own, hunting became more than a simple pastime. The mule-deer he brought home fed the kids, especially when money was tight, and money always seemed to be tight in those early years. There is almost nothing more exhilarating than when a hunter finally has a deer in his sights. Heart pounding and breath quickening, all the work and waiting culminates in the moment of taking the shot. Every skilled hunter understands the importance of selecting the proper positioning, adjusting the sights for accuracy, taking aim, breathing, and steadying themselves for successful follow through.

Allen approached starting a company like a skilled marksman. Every move he made was measured and methodical. He took time to strategize, secure a good starting position, and take careful aim. He analyzed what he needed to do to make the chance he was taking a successful one. He took time to steady himself, and he kept his plans relatively quiet until he was ready. Allen was determined to succeed because his wife and six young children were depending on him. However, he was equally determined to do things the right way. The man who once dug foundations knew he wanted Allen Lund Company to be built on the solid floor of honesty, transparency, and integrity.

After securing Kathie's blessing to strike out on his own, Allen exercised his commitment to transparency with his children. He sat them down to explain the decision he was making. He joked that he may need to dive into their piggy banks if things got really tight. David and Natalie, his two oldest children, were not keen on the idea of surrendering their babysitting and grass cutting money for the new business, and fortunately they would never have to do so. This may seem like a small gesture, explaining a decision of this magnitude to children who were too young to fully grasp the gravity of the choice their father was making. However, it illustrates perfectly the origins of the family-owned and family-focused company we see today. He would build ALC for them and involve his kids even at their early ages in the company's early stages.

Not everyone in the family was initially on board with Allen's plans. His mother, Maxine, cried for a week when she learned her son was going to quit his job. She lived through the Great Depression and saw children in their community starve. Maxine didn't want that for her grandchildren. She had also worked at the same bank for many years and couldn't imagine leaving a secure and steady job to take a risk like this. Her fear only subsided when Allen called to explain. Allen had carefully considered the risks and done the math. If he could book four loads a week, his children would eat. This satisfied his mother and quelled her worries.

Allen wanted to set himself up for a solid start. He knew a man named Jim Thornton who owned a small transportation brokerage company that did five or six loads a week. Jim was nearing retirement and agreed to let Allen buy the business from him for five thousand dollars. He would also stay and teach Allen the ropes for a few months. This would give Allen a solid footing to start on. Allen knew how to "speak trucker," and was confident he could keep those loads going and in time stretch it to ten loads a week.

Allen planned his exit and he didn't give any indication to the team at CH Robinson where he was going. He simply handed in his notice one day, keeping his next steps quiet. Allen didn't want to take clients away from CH Robinson. He didn't feel right about poaching any of their existing produce brokerage customers. He wanted to start by doing things the right way, and to him that meant a clean slate.

Kathie and Allen's youngest child, Christina, was nine months old at this time. Her Godparents, Karen and Dick Hurley, lived on Isabel street near the Lunds. The two families became fast friends. When work took the Hurleys to Hawaii for a few years, they invited Allen and Kathie to come out to their home on the island. Allen, having just quit his job, finally had a window of opportunity to get away. So Allen, Kathie, and Christina got on a plane to the islands for a ten-day vacation. The other children stayed home under the supervision of Allen's father, Wayne. Although David, who was fourteen at the time, ended up filling the role of the family caretaker since Wayne hurt his leg and was down and out for the week.

Allen knew he needed some rest to be able to start up again with strength. This pause would help him clear his mind and strategize his next steps. Allen also knew the trip would help signify the clean break he was making from CH Robinson, something that was very important to him.

Allen realized it would be a long time before his next vacation, once Allen Lund Company launched it would be full speed ahead from there. The quiet before the storm isn't easy to embrace when you know the storm is coming, and it wasn't easy for Allen Lund to sit still on a beach. He started the vacation committed to taking no phone calls, but the last three days he couldn't help but pick up the phone and start putting his carefully crafted plans into motion.

As soon as they returned to Los Angeles, Allen hit the ground running. He may have committed to not contacting any of CH Robinson's clients, but it didn't mean those clients didn't want to find him. People trusted Allen and liked doing business with him, and many clients were shocked to find out he had left. There were stacks of missed calls and messages waiting for him upon his return. He wouldn't take any of Robinson's previous produce customers, but all the connections Allen personally brought in only wanted to do business with him.

When news that Allen had gone out on his own reached the leadership in the Los Angeles office of CH Robinson, they were furious. They contacted their biggest truck line customers and threatened to blackball them from future work if they hauled any loads for Allen. Allen received calls from customers explaining the situation. E.D. Middleton, one of Allen's connections, called to apologize, explaining that Middleton had to adhere to Robinson's demands. His livelihood was at stake.

This heightened the difficulty of those early days for the new company, but it didn't slow Allen down. Allen's genuine respect for the truckers he worked with kept many loyal to him. He had made a habit of taking food and drinks to truckers he knew happened to be stuck waiting on delayed loads. Allen would bring food to the truck stops or he would take the truckers to dinner. Allen's love for people organically bred strong professional relationships. His kindness wasn't a means to an end, but it did end up benefiting him. The way he took care of people made people want to work with him. This was something no competitor could take away. Ironically, CH Robinson also couldn't tell any of the new clients Allen had brought in that they couldn't work with him. They didn't have personnel allocated to do what Allen had been doing for them on the transportation side of the business.

Things got very busy for Allen very quickly. He ended up loading twenty trucks in his first week. His first month, he booked one hundred loads. This far exceeded the four loads a week he needed to feed the kids. Cotton was a popular commodity at the time, grown in abundance in California. It needed to be shipped to textile mills in the southeastern region of the United States. These were some of Allen Lund Company's earliest loads. With only one thousand dollars in the bank to start out, Allen carefully chose customers he knew paid quickly, and trucking companies he knew invoiced slowly. Before the first trucking invoice came in, he had fifty thousand dollars in the bank and was ready to pay it. This was the start of a different life for Allen and his family.

Jim Thornton, the previous owner, didn't stay on after the first month. He was ready to retire and being astounded by the success Allen had, he didn't figure there was much more he could teach him. Jim left him the business and an old Plymouth duster, the company car, that went with it. No one predicted the radical and immediate success Allen would have. The president of CH Robinson flew to Los Angeles to meet with Allen. They would offer him a 100 percent raise if he would return, but Allen declined. This was the best thing for his family and his chance to carve out an entirely new company culture. After this CH Robinson drafted a non-compete clause to insulate themselves from the impact of future employees making an exodus. It was unofficially referred to as the "Allen Lund Non Compete Contract."

This animosity extended to physical space, as well. The Southern Pacific building hovered over the Downtown LA Produce Market. This beautiful historic building had been converted into leasable office spaces and only a third of the offices were full. Allen wanted to set up his office as soon as he returned from Hawaii. He reached out to the owner of the building, but the man wouldn't rent space to Allen. CH Robinson was Southern Pacific's biggest tenant, and they threatened to vacate their offices if the Allen Lund Company was allowed to set up shop in the building.

Allen instead decided to rent space in the dilapidated building directly across from the Southern Pacific. It wasn't much to look at, but Allen was able to get four hundred square feet for fifty dollars a month. For fun he would check in with the owner of Southern Pacific once a week just to see if he'd change his mind, but unsurprisingly the man never relented. Allen's small office was enough for him; he didn't have employees beyond the members of his own family.

Allen worked around the clock to get business flowing in, and Kathie supported him by keeping the books and paperwork up to date. Even the children were taught to answer the phone in a specific way. The Lunds never knew when a customer would call the house, so the children were taught a professional greeting. "Lund residence. David speaking. How can I help you?" was the template Allen gave his oldest son and it was passed down to all the kids. Calls about loads were coming in at all hours of the day and the whole family needed to be on board.

Allen initially chose the name Allen Lund Company because it was the logical choice. He needed people to recognize the name and immediately know who they were doing business with. However, years later he would second guess that decision. There was something about it that didn't feel humble to him. However, Allen Lund Company was the appropriate charter title. It was his name, network, and reputation that drew customers to him. His name was beginning to mean a great deal in the brokerage world. People wanted to do business with Allen Lund because he did things the right way. He treated truckers and customers with equal respect. He was a man of his word, and eventually as the company grew and employees were hired, he would treat them as if they were family too. The initial desire to feed his kids morphed into a calling to help feed all of the families of the people who worked for or with him. Every business decision he made was steeped in this calling, which led to quick expansion.

Despite the rapid changes there was one habit that endured from the earliest days of the company. Calls were very expensive to make then, so Allen had a reputation of keeping them brief and no-nonsense. Allen seldom said "Goodbye" to end a phone call. Goodbye was a filler word that felt like a waste of time and money. Instead, when ending calls Allen would say, "Be Good" and hang up. Those words were never a waste. The phrase was a reminder of how Allen oriented his life and a benediction for others to do the same.

CHAPTER ELEVEN

LITTLE LEAGUE WITH BIG EXPANSION

"I always count my blessings more than I count my money. I don't work for money, never did."

—*Dolly Parton*

Without Kathie Lund, Allen Lund could not have accomplished everything he was able to do. In the earliest days of the company, Kathie busied herself taking as much off of Allen's plate as possible. She knew that his gift was talking to people, selling services, and negotiating loads. Paperwork, filing, and accounting were things she could do to free Allen's time so he could lean into his gifts. She matched Allen in her energy and work ethic, and the two found harmony in appreciating each other's strengths.

Even the kids enjoyed helping out in the early days. On weekends Allen would bring his three oldest children downtown to see his work. David was fourteen, Natalie was thirteen, and Kenny was twelve by this time. On Saturday mornings, they would often get breakfast at Vickman's or The Pantry and then grab a haircut from Gomez, the barber whose shop was next to Allen's office. When they got to work, the kids cleaned the desks, took out the trash, and observed their father in his element. David, who had just started high school, was able to obtain a permit to officially work for his father. His jobs became more involved as he was tasked with painting, spraying the building for bugs, and organizing paperwork.

The kids loved going downtown, even if it was a seedy part of the city. Their Dad knew everyone and navigated the area with confidence. He did, however, keep an ax-handle in hand when walking to his car. For their protection, Allen had the kids carry it with them when they came in on the weekends. Though they felt safe with their dad in his office, the kids were terrified of the office building. It was run-down and falling apart. There was a rickety fire escape that scaled one side of the building and a dilapidated elevator that was pitch black when the doors closed. Kenny was afraid to ride the elevator and only wanted to take the stairs until the day he found a homeless man on one of the landings. After that encounter, Kenny would take his chances in the elevator.

The building wasn't ideal, but Allen soon became friends with many of the other tenants. Several men in the building also worked as transportation brokers for their own boutique companies. Among them were the DeWitt Brothers and a man named

Harold Felgar who swore like a sailor, kept a pet cockatoo, and always had a cigar hanging from his mouth that he chewed but never smoked. The group became unlikely companions. There was no cut-throat competition among them. In fact, it was the opposite. The men helped each other with loads and covered each other's phones when someone was out of the office. Allen believed there was enough business for all of them, and loved being in the same building as friends. Allen and Harold started hunting together during deer season in southeast Utah.

Even with all of the help from his friends and family, the rapidly growing business needed a workforce. The first hire was a secretary who could answer calls and take on the filing systems Kathie developed. Allen then hired three more salesmen who could broker deals.

Things were getting busy, but something unique about Allen Lund was his way of seeing time. On the shelf of his office, Allen kept a large jar that looked like a simple jar of rice (it remains on display at the company's corporate office to this day). The jar consists of fourteen walnuts and two and a half cups of rice. It all fits nicely inside, filling the jar to the rim. The jar is an illustration of a principle Allen Lund endeavored to live. If someone poured the rice in first and then tried to add the walnuts, there would be no way to fit the walnuts into the jar. However, if the walnuts are added first, followed by the rice, all of the materials fit perfectly together as the rice fills the empty seams between the walnuts. In the metaphor, the walnuts represent the most important things God has for us to do. The rice represents everything else we need to get done or want to do. The jar was a reminder to Allen to prioritize the most important things. If he placed God's callings first, he would always have plenty of time for the rest.

Business was important to him, but never at the expense of being there for his family. Fatherhood was a "walnut." Allen understood the importance of being involved in his kids' lives and he always wanted to be a part of the things they were doing. Starting his work days so early in the morning allowed him to use a lot of afternoons and evenings to invest time in them.

All of the Lund kids played sports growing up, but baseball and softball were the primary pastimes. Allen would often joke that all other sports existed to keep you in shape for baseball. He loved spending time watching the sport and knew the game backward and forward. So when the kids went out for their little league and softball teams, Allen became their coach.

Allen was the kind of coach who encouraged you but also expected you to work hard. Effort and attitude were paramount. Everything else from talent to technique could get built up or ironed out through hard work. He was excellent at helping kids perfect their swing. He'd take extra time in the batting cages with a player to ensure they got it just right. When he coached the boys in Little League he was part of a handful of parents who formed the coaching staff. When Natalie started playing softball, he was the assistant coach. Coaching girls was a whole new ballgame for Allen, but he was equally dedicated to their teams. They made him laugh a lot and he teased them just like he did the boys. Everyone could tell if Allen liked someone because he would tease the people he liked the most.

Allen was extremely invested in his kids' education and always showed up at every important event. All three of Allen's sons attended St. Francis High School in La Canada, a private all-boys school run by Franciscan Friars. Kenny was the most talkative and energetic of the kids, which also meant his teachers sometimes had difficulty getting him to sit still and pay attention. Ken Deasy, a Franciscan brother who taught Kenny at St. Francis couldn't wait for Parent Teacher Conference Day, when he could finally let Kenny's parents hear all of his complaints. When the conference began, Brother Ken was shocked by the six-foot-four burly and imposing figure of Allen Lund walking into the room. Allen sat down and asked how his son was doing in class, and the friar changed his tune completely, squeaking out something to the effect of Kenny being a model student and how he was doing "just fine."

Allen could be very intimidating to people when they first met him. Beyond his size, he had a sharp mind and direct way of communicating. Yet Allen loved getting to know people, especially the people in his children's lives. He'd eventually form a lot of friendships with the Franciscan Friars who ran the school, including Brother Ken. Then Allen would hear more accurate reports on his sons' academic endeavors. He expected all of his children to do well and get good grades, but the subjects he cared the most about were religion and behavior. Allen felt that if his children were getting a solid foundation in their faith, and showing good character towards their teachers and peers, then everything else would fall into place for them. Their academic strengths would soon show themselves if these two pillars were solid.

Showing up for his family and making sure the company was doing well so that his employees could also be in positions to show up for their own families were the guideposts that kept Allen Lund Company moving forward. Business and family never competed. They ran parallel to each other like train tracks. The more Allen invested time in one, the more the other benefitted. A perfect example of this was Allen's decision to move his office from downtown LA to where it is today.

Allen loved being downtown near the produce market, but he didn't like how unsafe it was for his family and employees going to work. He decided to start looking for office space elsewhere. During this time, David was in high school at St. Francis and Natalie was in school at Flintridge Sacred Heart Academy. Both schools were located in La Canada. Allen was a coach on Natalie's softball team, and all of the time spent there made him familiar with that part of northern Los Angeles.

In 1979, construction was completed on a section of the 210 Freeway that runs along the northern perimeter of the San Fernando Valley flanked by the San Gabriel mountains. It was designed to alleviate tractor-trailer traffic from major through-ways. Both the 210 freeway and the Angeles Crest Freeway run through La Canada near St. Francis School. Allen realized this would be the perfect location for his company because it would give truckers who needed to pick up their payment easy access to come into their office. There was space for them to park their trucks on the overpass bridge and walk down the ramp to the office to pick up their checks. As a bonus, being in La Canada would also put him in closer proximity to his kids. On March 13, 1979 Allen Lund signed a lease for Room 315, a 1,500 square foot space in an office building near the intersection of the two freeways. They would soon outgrow the office as business continued to expand and new employees were hired. Fortunately, other tenants in the building periodically moved out of their office spaces; and each time Allen would take over those offices as well.

Eventually, Allen Lund Company had employees in every office in the building. Allen would buy the entire property, making it the corporate headquarters of ALC. Allen wasn't just growing his business in Los Angeles. Branch offices were started in different parts of the country.

The first branch office opened in Atlanta in April of 1978. Allen wanted to ensure that all of his employees could feel like they had a stake in the company. Every satellite office became its own entrepreneurial venture, keeping a generous portion of the profits they earned each quarter. The manager decided how to share this bonus with their employees. Human resources, accounting, IT, and marketing departments were hosted at the corporate office and handled business for all the offices nationwide. Similar to those early days when Kathie freed Allen's time to focus on sales, this meant the managers and their teams could focus their efforts on bringing in business and getting those jobs done well. Each office would pay the same percentage to the headquarters for these services. However, Allen left decisions on how the branch managers budgeted the remainder of the revenue entirely up to them. Each office also had its own profit and loss statement. This made the offices independent from each other, and the managers were treated like entrepreneurs.

Before a new office opened, Allen would fly out to meet with that prospective manager. The meetings were brief because Allen could get a good read on people quickly. He wouldn't just talk to them about business. Allen mainly wanted to know about that person's life, family, and attitude toward their employees. Allen needed to be able to trust the person's character above all else. He was very selective of the managers he hired. Allen never started another office until he found the right people to place at the helm. People were more important than strategic shipping locations. He had a specific way of doing business and wanted managers who also exemplified honesty, a commitment to excellence, and a commitment to treating their teams well. If Allen was satisfied upon meeting a manager, they would shake hands and Allen would catch a flight home that same day. His office in Los Angeles was still very young, so he didn't have the luxury of too much time away.

Expansion is a tricky stage for any company to navigate. Many companies have gone off the rails for expanding too quickly. Often they overextend themselves financially or they face a crisis of company culture and the overall quality of their services deteriorate. This wasn't the case for Allen Lund because he handled expansion differently than most. In the early days, Allen would wait until a new office became profitable before opening another. Although he would become more aggressive in later years, this steady growth was Allen's way of ensuring they never overextended themselves. Beyond temperance, Allen also had a gift for bringing people together. He committed to knitting inward as things were expanding outward. He would bring new managers and employees to California and invite them into his home. He wanted to get to know them and be able to communicate his heart for the company face to face.

He also started an in-person annual managers meeting so good ideas could cross-pollinate among the offices. He spent hours each day reading reports from each office and built transparency into the company culture. The branch offices could see where corporate overhead funds were allocated. The managers could also see the reports of other offices so they could regularly grow and learn from each other.

Offices sprang up around the country, but Allen refused to expand to Salt Lake City. Roger Lowe, Allen's friend who gave him his start at CH Robinson, was still in business in Salt Lake and Allen refused to compete with Roger. Plans for an Allen Lund Company office in this region would only start once Roger had retired. This was how Allen did business. It wasn't about the money for him; it was about remaining loyal to his friends, partners, and employees.

As expansion continued, Allen found ways to organically engage all of his children in the company. His son David was still working for him on the weekends while in high school. As all high schoolers do, David started to dream about what was next for him. Initially, David wanted to be an Air Force pilot, but his eyesight didn't meet the strict criteria. David had also inherited his father's height, which was a second strike against this dream. Allen encouraged David to attend Glendale Community College because they had an aviation program. David completed his ground school there during his senior year of high school. Not long after David got his pilot's license, Allen bought a company airplane.

While in college, David flew his father to meet with customers all over California and became the company's first unofficial part-time pilot. Air travel saved Allen time, but it also gave him another way of connecting with his son and incorporating David's skills and interests into the company dynamic. They had a lot of fun together, and per Allen's request, stopped to refuel at the airports that had good restaurants. One of their favorite places to refuel was Harris Ranch, where the father-son duo would grab a steak dinner before taking off again.

Allen's lifelong love of machinery easily transitioned to airplanes. He began to study planes and enjoyed discussing the minutiae of each model with the mechanics at the hanger. He ordered pilot's magazines and became a maven of aviation, but he never flew himself. He never asked to take the yoke to steer, even for a moment. Flying was David's dream and Allen was content to be with him for it. Fueling the lives of his children would shape the company as much as the company shaped them. While many experts lecture on the principles of work-life balance, looking at the life of Allen Lund reveals the greatest lesson of all. Allen's mission was always centered on helping other people grow and excel. The clarity of this mission simplified his decision-making and kept his life and work in perfect harmony. However, Allen was able to do this because he never saw it as a balancing act, with a fear of one thing toppling the other. Allen had one focus that forged his way forward, and that was doing the right thing by all the people he knew. During his career, people marveled at Allen's ability to get things done, wondering how on earth he found time in the day to do it all. Yet, just like the jar he kept in his office, Allen simply kept the things God would want him to do first in his life, and everything else seemed to fit together just right.

CHAPTER TWELVE
FROM RUSSIA WITH LOVE

"When wealth is lost, nothing is lost. When health is lost, something is lost. When character is lost, everything is lost."

—*Billy Graham*

Allen's youngest son, Eddie Lund, shared his father's love for baseball and had a special talent for the sport. Eddie was extremely competitive and would get emotionally invested in what happened on the field. At twelve, he was pitching a game that wasn't going his team's way. Frustration mounted and Eddie lost his temper, making several angry gestures to the umpire. Allen watched from the stands and was very quiet on the drive home.

Allen finally broke his silence, "If you ever do that again, you will be off this team."

Those were the only words he had to say on the matter, and they were enough. Eddie knew his father never made empty threats. He also knew that he had disappointed him, something none of Allen's children ever wanted to do. They respected their father and knew that showing good character was what their father expected. Eddie seldom lost his temper on the field again, and Allen's words changed him as a player. He never needed to learn to pump himself up for a game, but he did learn to regulate his emotions which would serve him for years to come on and off the field.

Exhibiting strong moral character was important to Allen, first because it was simply the right thing to do, and second because Allen understood just how far reputation could take you. For Allen, reputation was the foundation of trust people had in your name, and it was his name that allowed him to secure customers in the early days of his business.

Blue Book Services is a credit-rating directory service that has been providing information to the produce industry since 1901. Each year they would print a physical directory listing all the businesses related to produce from sellers to brokers. Blue Book would assign an "X" rating to each company based on several metrics. They would evaluate the company's financial stability, their record of paying invoices on time, reviews among their industry peers, and the number of disputes in which they were involved, if any. A three "X" score was considered good and a four "X" score was excellent.

Allen knew how important it was to get listed in the Blue Book right away. It would allow more customers to find Allen

Lund Company and give them credibility in the industry. ALC became one of the youngest companies to earn a four "X" rating. Their reputation was solidified in the produce industry as a truck broker you could trust with your product.

Allen also used the Blue Book to vet other businesses he worked with. He would get calls from businesses needing trucks for their loads and consulted Blue Book to find out who they were and what their reputation was like. He didn't do business with sellers with a rating lower than three "X." It wasn't worth the risk to Allen. He was far too protective of the truckers and the mom-and-pop-owned trucking companies with whom he did business. There are 400,000 trucking companies in the United States. Ninety-two percent of those companies own five or fewer trucks. Ninety-seven percent of them own fewer than twenty. This means most trucking companies are small family-owned businesses. Allen, who was actively building his own family business, wanted to make sure these truckers were taken care of and never put in a bad situation.

Blue Book helped Allen keep his finger on the pulse of the industry, and business was booming more than ever. Deregulation began under the Carter Administration in the early 1980s and continued after Ronald Reagan was sworn in as President in 1981. Before this, brokers could only haul "exempt" commodities: produce, cotton, nursery stock, etc. You couldn't coordinate loads for manufactured products. This changed with deregulation, opening the industry to a wealth of new possibilities. Now Allen could do business with anyone who needed to put anything on a truck. Even still, Allen maintained a fairly conservative approach to growth. His goal was to grow the business 10 to 15 percent each year. This was manageable and ensured that the integrity and excellence the company had become known for could be maintained as the company grew.

Despite deregulation, Allen also kept his business primarily focused on food and fiber. Allen said no matter what ebbs and flows came with an ever-changing economy, people would always need to buy food and clothes. Keeping a healthy portion of their loads in produce and cotton stabilized the company over the years. Allen believed in steady growth, never over-extending their finances or going into debt, and making sure they did the small things right. Good stewards of the small things could be trusted with bigger ones, so every interaction with his customers was important.

Allen particularly loved interacting with the truckers. He would often joke with them about how they had it easy. When he was young, there were no automatic transmissions and the trucker had to do all their own vehicle maintenance. All jesting aside, Allen had high standards for the truckers he did business with. He expected them to conduct themselves professionally while on the job. Allen had a CB radio installed in his car so he could listen and communicate with trucks on the road. He was aghast when he would hear them using foul language over the comms.

"Can you imagine airline pilots speaking that way?" Allen rebuked them. He had young children in the backseat whose ears he wanted to protect, but he also wanted to raise the standards of an industry he loved. The personal relationships he developed with these trucking companies paid off when the trucking market was tight. Allen Lund Company always grew during seasons when it was difficult to secure trucks because truckers in high demand chose to haul for Allen over his competitors. Treating them well, down to the smallest business dealing, earned their loyalty.

Allen Lund Company had become financially successful, which came with a new array of challenges. A truck carrying a load they had brokered got into an accident involving several cars. To the lawyers involved, ALC was a fattened calf ready for barbecuing. They sued everyone they could over the accident, including the Allen Lund Company. Allen was baffled. Suing a broker for a truck involved in an accident was akin to a person suing their travel agent for their cruise ship running aground. After taking depositions, the insurance company settled the lawsuit quickly out of court, but the incident bothered Allen. He created a new department that vetted and monitored trucks more extensively, realizing he needed to screen them for their reputations as much as he was screening the sellers.

Allen realized legislation protecting brokers needed to be put in place to guard them from lawsuits like this one. Allen had previously become a member of the TBCA, Truck Brokers Conference of America. Joining this organization increased your legitimacy in the industry and the group lobbied on behalf of brokers. Allen became a board member, and soon after Chair of the Board of Directors. Allen and the early pioneers on the board included industry greats like Bill Hay, William J. Augello, Boe Davis, Jerry Gereghty, Bill Tucker, Charles McAlpin, and Thomas A. Fiorini. Together they rebranded their organization to be the TIA, Transportation Intermediaries Association. This broadened their membership base from what was exclusively brokers to include warehouses, international shippers, and freight forwarders. Unifying these facets of the transportation industry strengthened the organization and would raise standards across the board. Under Allen's leadership, they moved the organization from Chicago to Washington DC so they could better work on legislation that enabled fair practices and expanded the industry.

The TIA offers members educational seminars and networking opportunities where they can learn from their peers in the industry. Allen specifically developed a program called Broker's Bootcamp that taught new brokers the tricks of the trade. They would travel to different cities across America giving these lectures. Allen knew he was effectively training his own competition, but he felt there was enough room in the business for everyone. So he was committed in his efforts to improve the industry as a whole. Most importantly, Allen carried the conviction that membership in this organization needed to be meaningful. Being a part of the TIA should say something about the efficacy of your business, so he worked to create an ethics statement that everyone joining the organization had to sign. The ethics statement remains a requirement for TIA membership to this day. Just like a high tide causes all of the boats in a harbor to rise together, Allen wanted to see the industry at large improve. So he was generous with the time, information, and advice he shared with TIA members. Allen believed there was enough room in this business for everyone, and in his opinion a business's primary objective was to improve the lives of people.

* * *

In 1987, President Ronald Reagan gave a famous speech in front of the Brandenburg Gate in Berlin, Germany. "Mr. Gorbachev, tear down this wall," were the famous words that embodied the Western world's pressure on the leadership of the U.S.S.R. to open up its doors to democratization. In 1991, the Soviet Union's collapse freed its citizens from the grip of communism. But the political and economic transitions came quickly, out-pacing the ability of new governments to create the necessary capitalist economic infrastructure that people in the U.S. take for granted. Russia and other countries formerly dominated by communism, newly free but ill-prepared, plunged into dire economic conditions. Millions of people became impoverished. The political upheaval created a power vacuum that was filled in many places by the Russian Mafia. At the time, there were over eight hundred criminal organizations in Russia who formed an extensive black market network.

In 1992, the United States Department of Agriculture put together a task force of advisors to go to Moscow to help establish a better food distribution system. At the time, over 50 percent of Russian produce was lost in transportation. There were many issues with the supply chains including poor infrastructure, inefficient logistics, and no accountability for drivers who didn't bring in their loads in proper condition.

Allen Lund was selected to be a part of the team that went to Russia. His time working with the TIA in Washington D.C. put him on the USDA's radar. He would work alongside academics, politicians, and other business leaders to help solve these issues. Their primary goal was to get good produce to the eleve million people in Moscow.

Allen generously stepped away from his company for three months to go on this mission. He quickly became fascinated by the country and its people. Due to the expense of international calls, Allen wasn't able to talk to his family often during this time period. So he decided to keep a journal of his many adventures in Russia. He felt a great sense of purpose in using his God-given gifts and vast experience to help a country rebuild after decades of turmoil. While there, Allen was able to work with Russian farmers who were delighted to be introduced to new crops and western techniques. Allen had great confidence in the farmers and their ability to grow anything.

Farmers and truckers alike discovered quickly that Allen was not some optimistic bureaucrat. In one example, a trucker was having a difficult time backing his truck up to a loading dock. Allen jumped in the truck and did it for him. Allen could roll up his sleeves, drive the big rigs, and whip just about anything into shape. He and the team restructured the supply chains to get food to customers more efficiently. However, Allen soon discovered that the issues they were trying to solve were deeper than logistics. Poverty can be extremely dehumanizing, and decades of communism had stripped many Russians of a sense of dignity and personal pride in their work.

On another occasion, a truck carrying cabbage arrived at the produce market. The cabbage had spoiled because the driver sold the diesel fuel that ran the trailer's refrigeration unit on the black market along his route. This was a common practice, and at the time there was no accountability for how the loads came in. The diesel fuel tank for the refrigeration unit was separate from the tank of diesel fuel that ran the truck's engine. He left with plenty of diesel for the trip in the refrigeration unit and came back with none. The truck driver knew he would be paid whether or not the food spoiled, so he thought he might as well get twice the payday. What made the driver an equivalent of twenty dollars on the black market ruined twenty-thousand dollars worth of produce. Through translators, Allen was able to understand what had happened and his frustration peaked.

Allen picked up a metal pipe and announced to the translators he was going to kill the driver. The translators and Russian warehouse operators descended into chaos. The driver cowered behind the warehouse manager who begged Allen in broken English to not resort to violence. Of course, Allen had no intention of actually hurting anyone, but he decided to put the fear of God into the man. He yelled that as a trucker his load was his responsibility, and taking food off of the plates of starving people was a grievous sin deserving of death. He then dropped the metal pipe and walked away from the trembling trucker. Allen later explained to the warehouse manager that he wanted to convey a strong message to the man and the industry as a whole that actions like this should no longer be tolerated. The truckers would need to be responsible and accountable for the condition of their loads upon arrival.

Some of the ideas Allen implemented in Russia became a success, but Allen learned that progress was often a slower process than one hoped. In Moscow, the team helped a grocery set up a demonstration in their store of a western way of shopping for produce. Groceries in Russia had enormous lines because customers would grab a ticket for each item they wished to purchase and present it to a cashier who would then go and select the items for them filling their cart. Allen set up the demonstration to allow customers to do their own shopping. The customers were delighted to have the freedom to select their own items rather than be relegated to accepting whatever cabbage someone chose for them. Making their own selections was a small but empowering act. This cut down the lines, excited the clientele, increased the amount of produce sold, and made the grocery more profitable.

However, days later when Allen returned to the store, he was saddened to see them return to the old system of doing things. Their rationale was that there was no way they could trust customers to go through the aisles and make their own selections. They feared it would leave them open to theft and chaos. Allen grieved that it seemed an entire generation of Russians were lost to this fear-based mindset. They were still being victimized by communism because it had stolen their entrepreneurial spirit and belief in their fellow man.

Allen, however, was encouraged while observing the younger generation of Russians who hustled and sold in the open air markets anything they could. Hope for the country rested with those youths who still possessed an indomitable spirit.

During his three months in Russia, Allen poured heart, time, and resources into doing as much good as he could in the country. There are few CEOs who would be willing to step away from their companies for that amount of time, simply to help people in need. Allen also went above and beyond the call of the task force in his efforts to aid the Russian people. At the produce market employees were using abacuses for adding as they made transactions. He asked the translators why they didn't use adding machines or calculators and they explained it was too risky without consistent power and batteries were too expensive. The next day Allen placed an international call to his office in La Canada and had them send boxes of solar powered calculators to Moscow. Allen personally took on the expense.

Allen would go the extra mile to see people succeed. He sacrificed time to be in Russia, but Allen knew that beyond the principles of reaping what you sow, it was impossible to outgive God. Though he never expected a blessing for his own company to come from this trip, one of the other members of the task force, a produce retailer named Ben Capilouto, became close to Allen while working with him in Russia. Ben was older and smaller in stature. Allen watched out for Ben as they navigated Moscow, protecting him from pick-pockets and seedy characters. Ben respected and trusted Allen. When Ben got back to the states he was hired to set up a brand new produce sector for Costco. Ben recommended that Costco use the Allen Lund Company to manage the transportation of these produce loads. This was the start of a now thirty-year relationship between the two companies.

Even in Russia, Allen's reputation in the industry grew stronger. A few months after returning to the United States, Allen had some of his contacts from Russia fly into California for business. They were a part of the Russian contingent that operated the produce distribution center in Moscow. Allen proposed that there may be an opportunity for them to export specialty produce items that were conducive to growing in California's climate.

Allen picked them up from the airport and took them, their wives, and their translators to Disneyland. Allen drove one car and his son Kenny drove the other. They had a wonderful day, but on the drive back to Los Angeles the women cried. Kenny asked the translators what was wrong and they explained that the wives couldn't believe a place like that existed, simply for enjoyment. They explained that in Russia people stood in line to get food, and in America they stood in line to have fun. They felt they had been lied to about the United States, and they cried because none of their friends back home would ever believe the things they told them about this trip. After years under the oppression of communism, they saw things in America they found difficult to put into words, and they grieved for all the time they had been kept from knowing what life could be like when people are free.

CHAPTER THIRTEEN

HAULING YOUR OWN

"Do you wish to rise? Begin by descending. You plan a tower that will pierce the clouds? Lay first the foundation of humility."

—*St. Augustine*

Part of the reason Allen was able to step away from his company for three months was because his eldest son David was managing the LA office. David worked part-time for his dad throughout college. He did every odd job around the office he could find, flew Allen to meet with customers, and learned the specific cadence of making a sale from observing his father in action. When David graduated, Allen put him on the sales floor as a broker.

At that time, brokering was an entry-level position at ALC. Being a broker would give David the foundational knowledge he needed to grow within the company. He became the manager of the Los Angeles office soon after. Though David was now managing, his office was right next to Allen's and there was only a sliding glass window separating them. So Allen could hear everything his son was saying on calls. There were many suggestions and reminders Allen would give his son as he mentored him in his new position.

Allen was immensely proud to have his son working for him. This was part of the vision he had tirelessly labored to bring to fruition. Allen could have done very well without growing the company to the extent he did. If he wanted to simply create a good life for himself and his wife with a solid retirement fund, he could have easily done so with a handful of loads each month. Though well aware of this, Allen derived joy from being able to create opportunities for people. Building the company meant providing more people with good jobs. His children would also have the opportunity to take part in the business if they chose.

Although the invitation to join the company was there for them, Allen never insisted they follow that path. As a father, Allen gave his children a lot of freedom to make their own decisions about where they wanted to go to college, what they wanted to study, and what career paths excited them the most. He did, however, repeat one phrase to them all: "Eighteen and out!"

All of the Lund children knew what that meant. At eighteen years of age, Allen and Kathie expected their children to go to college; and they were not allowed to live at home during their studies. As parents, they wanted their kids to experience the world and learn independence. "Eighteen and out" was part of that protocol.

For a man who never went to college, Allen had enormous faith in higher education. He put all six of his children through school, providing for their tuition and living needs. He wanted each of them to use those collegiate years to focus on learning and discovery. Work would be there for them when they got out. Before his son Kenny left for college, Allen took him to lunch. When Kenny asked his father for advice, Allen had only this to say: "Go to church every week and everything else will work out alright." Simple but profound, those words guided Kenny through the years.

When Kenny graduated, he decided to go in a different direction than his brother David. Kenny taught high school and coached baseball during the school year and worked as a camp director in the summers. He spent three years doing this before he decided it was time for a change. Then he ended up standing in Allen's office asking for a job.

"I'm going to give you every lousy job there is to do in this office, otherwise the people here will never respect you," Allen explained to Kenny.

Simply being a Lund was not enough to earn privileges in the company. If anything, Allen's children had to work a lot harder than most to prove they were ready to take on more responsibilities. They would need to start at the bottom and work their way up. Allen made good on his promise to keep Kenny busy with all the odd tasks that needed doing around the office. Like

David before him, Kenny cleaned, painted, changed every light bulb, and on several occasions found himself crawling around the attic running computer cables throughout the building.

In one instance, starting at the bottom and working up became very literal for Kenny, who was tasked with fixing the elevator at the La Canada office. It often fell out of sequence and needed to be reset. Allen didn't want to pay a repairman to fix something he was confident he and Kenny could do themselves. So Allen would go into the breaker room in the basement where the elevator controls were, bypass the sign reading "Warning: High Voltage," and press down the individual levers with a pencil as Kenny rode the elevator and pushed the interrelated buttons. The elevator lurched up and down violently. When the doors opened on the top floor, an unsuspecting tenant hopped in the elevator with Kenny, who didn't have time to shout a warning before the doors slammed behind her. They heard a series of unsettling mechanical noises. The woman, whose face was now white with fear, ran out of the elevator as soon as the doors opened again. She turned around and watched Kenny, still inside, slowly sinking from the landing and disappearing out of sight, with the elevator doors still open.

Eventually, Allen and Kenny were able to get the system back in sequence. The comical anecdote is a microcosm of a principle Allen instilled in his children: see if you can figure out a solution, try things, and be resourceful. This doctrine imbued the Lund children with independence and confidence. It was an appendage to Allen's "eighteen and out" philosophy. For any parent, there is a duel between two coexisting desires. One desire is to raise well-adjusted children, who grow to become independent. The other desire is to keep your children close to you. In these, Allen struck a balance by simply being present as his kids followed their own paths and passions.

The youngest Lund son, Eddie, continued his baseball career at the University of Notre Dame. Eddie's senior year, Allen invested in a condo across from campus so he could attend all his son's games. He rented the condo out during football season and worked remotely at the condo during baseball season, occasionally taking Eddie out to dinner, but otherwise keeping a low profile. The goal wasn't to impede Eddie's independence. Allen simply loved his son and wanted to watch him play. He also supported Eddie's baseball career after graduation as he went on to play for the LA Dodgers, spending four years in the minor leagues.

Allen worked to build and sustain a close relationship with all his children. Allen telephoned each of his daughters daily to check on them. He also always wanted to be the one to drop them off or pick them up from the airport when they traveled. Allen knew everyone's travel itinerary and often parked his truck nearby to watch their planes land. When his children touched down, they could see that truck and knew their father was watching and waiting for them.

When his youngest child, Christina, was leaving to study abroad in Europe for a year, Allen negotiated with the phone company to get a good rate that would allow her to call home as often as she wanted. Christina was nervous about being away from home for so long. She packed her bags and went to say goodbye to her parents who were both working at the office that day. Christina was extremely emotional and wondered if she was making the right choice to go at all. Kathie opened up Christina's itinerary and read aloud all of the exciting places she was about to see.

Optimistic and practical in her thinking, Kathie assured her, "Your father and I have never seen any of these places, you're blessed, so go have fun."

Allen, in contrast, was just as emotional as Christina. He drove her to the airport, walked her to the gate, and was teary-eyed while giving her a farewell hug. Often in situations where emotions were running high, Allen would joke, "Don't come in here with your hair on fire." In business, he was great at lightening a moment that way and expert at keeping his composure. However, the love Allen felt for his children was palpable. He loved them wholeheartedly and unreservedly, so there were moments like this when his raw emotions spilled over.

Allen structured his company with the same principles he

built into the family dynamic. He wanted his children to grow and gain independence, but he also wanted to make sure there was a strong connection and healthy line of communication between them, no matter the distance. They were independent, but supported. He built his company the same way. Allen felt the role of the corporate office was to bolster the branches, not the other way around. He wanted each branch office to maintain independence as its own entrepreneurial entity, but he knew he also needed to keep them close to the heart of the company. His time working at CH Robinson taught Allen just how different various offices could be. Even though they were part of the same company, working with Roger Lowe in Utah had been a completely different experience than working for the CH Robinson office in downtown Los Angeles. They didn't conduct business the same way. This lack of cohesive company culture bothered Allen, and he knew he needed to ensure every ALC office stayed on brand. Investing in cutting-edge technological advancements made this possible.

Allen loved to figure out how machines worked. Similar to the elevator, Allen always tried to fix things. In another life, he would've been a great mechanic because he loved restoring old engines. This was his hobby and he was even in a group dedicated to the pastime: The Hit & Miss Club. They'd head out together and restore early gasoline engines, repurposing them to grind things like flour and cornmeal. Then they would display them for people to view at Knotts Berry Farm for their old farm day festivals. Working with his hands on projects like this gave Allen a lot of satisfaction. He also loved purchasing gadgets and his ever-curious mind enjoyed reading about new innovations.

When fax machines came on the scene, Allen insisted every ALC office purchase one. There were some dissenting opinions about this, with several managers feeling this was an unnecessary expense. But Allen saw it as an investment in the future of communication that would eventually put them ahead of the competition.

Allen's friend Dick Hurley was influential in shaping Allen's understanding of new technologies that improved business capability. The Hurley's lived on Isabel Street by Allen and Kathie. They were Christina's Godparents and the couple the Lunds went to Hawaii with before starting their business. Dick Hurley worked for National Cash Register and that company was making a transition to computer and software sales. He would regularly discuss the future of technology with Allen. All the distribution systems and warehouses were going to eventually be run on computers. The Commodore 64 and Basic/Four computers had recently hit the market, and larger companies were beginning their transition to the digital world.

Up to this point, brokers were typing up orders using typewriters on triplicate forms. In the early days of the company, Kathie came up with a filing system that kept all of the necessary information about a load on the front of each file jacket. That way, an employee could get all of the data they needed with a quick glance rather than digging through the file. Fully convinced that Dick Hurley was right about the new technological direction the business world was leaning, Allen computerized his company. He was one of the first CEOs in the industry to do so. Dick Hurley helped Allen purchase the first mainframe from a startup company called Rexon. This made Allen Lund Company more efficient with accounts receivable, accounts payable, and all other bookkeeping systems. The improvements made them effective in serving larger corporate customers.

Each employee had a computer monitor on their desk to process all the information on a truckload, manage invoices, and pay truckers. As there was no software available for a truck brokerage, David worked with a programmer who took a distribution software package and adapted it to fit the needs of ALC. This was the first truck brokerage program to be designed on a mainframe computer. They digitized the system Kathie developed, creating electronic file jackets that displayed the key details of each load on the monitors. All offices used the same software system, making the transfer of information seamless.

Computers were a huge financial investment for Allen, but they paid off. Innovation resulted in growth. At that time the company's largest expense, second only to payroll, was long-distance calls. AT&T cornered the market as everyone's service provider, allowing them to charge high prices for phone calls: $0.50 per minute. For a brokerage company that conducted most of its business over the phone with offices across the United States, remotely negotiating loads and communicating with trucks moving on interstates in every direction, that phone bill was a daunting figure that had Allen searching for alternatives.

In 1984, the U.S. Department of Justice broke up the AT&T Corporation monopoly, insisting they relinquish control of the Bell Companies which provided service for local calls across America. This created opportunities for smaller companies to throw their hat in the phone service ring. MCI was the second largest long-distance telephone company in the United States, in direct competition with AT&T. They had developed some new technology that was able to cut Allen's phone bill in half.

In the early 1990s, MCI introduced Allen to frame relay technology. Frame relay would allow Allen Lund Company to create its own private network. It connected all phones and computers in each office to the same network that ran 24/7. This meant every call or fax sent between any of the Allen Lund Company offices, regardless of their geographical location, was free. With this technology, Allen would be able to easily conference call with his managers. Allen took the risk to see if this technology could work for them. The first installation of the updated phone system was a fifty thousand dollar purchase. Allen needed someone to oversee the rapid implementation of new technology into his business. Having graduated from grunt work and survived elevator repairs, Kenny, who had a natural propensity for technology, became the company's first IT employee.

For the frame relay technology to work, every branch office needed to install a T1 high-speed phone line. Kenny traveled to every ALC office to wire them into the network. The new system was a roaring success. Not only did it save Allen Lund Company a significant amount of money, it also brought about the desired effect of keeping all of the offices connected and on brand with the way Allen believed in doing business. Part of the mission of Allen Lund Company is to recruit and train the best employees in the industry. Allen understood for that to happen he needed to equip his employees with the best tools available. His commitment to staying on the cutting-edge of new technologies was rooted in his belief that his role as CEO was to support the branch offices and give them everything they needed to stay ahead of the competition.

Kenny may have started doing "every lousy job" around the office, but now he would begin to build an entire IT department at Allen Lund Company. Eventually, the Rexon computers would be replaced with Microsoft desktops. Kenny would oversee all the company's technological innovations in a rapidly changing world. For Allen, however, technology was simply akin to keeping that glass window in his office open so he could hear his son's work and stay connected to what was happening on the sales floor. Allen was keenly aware of the people he loved, wanting to know everything that was going on with them. He was this way with his family as well as his employees, who all became like family to him.

All three of Allen's sons ended up working for the company. They all started as brokers and worked their way up to management. David ran the LA office, Kenny headed the IT Department, and Eddie became a manager in the San Antonio office after working as assistant manager in the Portland office. In 2004, Allen made each of them vice presidents of the company. Kenny became the VP of Support Departments, and David and Eddie became Vice Presidents of Sales and Operations, a promotion that would eventually require Eddie to move back to Los Angeles.

Allen's vision for a cohesive, well-connected, and family-owned company was taking shape. All three Lund daughters would eventually sit on the Board of Directors. Christina's husband, Steve, who she met on that year-long trip studying abroad, would become an employee of Allen Lund Company, starting as an intern and working his way up to CFO. Natalie's husband, Kirk, a Delta pilot, also ended up working for Allen as the company's official pilot. Allen's initial desire to feed his kids was now allowing his children to do the same for their own families.

CHAPTER FOURTEEN
YOUR WORLD, I'M LIVING IN IT

"The American dream is that every man must be free to become whatever God intends he should become."

—Ronald Reagan

Allen loved meeting new people wherever he went. It was easy for him to make friends because he had a relentlessly curious mind. He'd strike up conversations, asking about their jobs, lives, and interests. In a world where many individuals are focused on the minutiae of their own lives, Allen took an interest in others. He was always passively scouting for talent. He'd frequently hire new people who impressed him with hard work or good customer service skills, offering several waitresses and bank tellers jobs on the spot. They would show up at the office the next day and no one knew who they were until they meekly explained that a very tall man named Allen had hired them. They were then brought to the Human Resources Department to get onboarded.

Friendly but discerning, Allen could get a read on people

quickly. In official job interviews, he wasn't just interested in a candidate's business experience. He also wanted to get a feel for their character. He would ask questions about their families and their passions outside of work. Most of all, when interviewing potential new managers, he wanted to know how committed they were to taking care of their employees.

Allen Lund Company was building a strong reputation in the industry, even among its competitors. As the company continued to expand, many smaller brokerages wanted to become new branch locations of Allen Lund Company. They knew they'd still be able to operate with a lot of independence, but with the enormous network and support the ALC corporate office could give them. On one occasion, when Allen was considering one of these acquisitions, he flew out to meet with the potential new manager. Most of the questions Allen had for him were about his team. Allen kept circling back the conversation to questions about the employees, despite the manager wanting to talk about his fiscal accomplishments. The candidate finally stopped the interview, bluntly asking: "Why do you keep asking about my employees? I can always hire new ones."

Needless to say, those words were the nail-in-the-coffin that brought the unsuccessful interview to a close. If there was one thing Allen was serious about, it was taking care of the people who worked for him. That was paramount to good leadership, so Allen would vet his managers for these qualities. Once he felt confident he had hired the right person, he would then step back and trust them with the reins to run their team.

Allen wanted people to feel they had ownership of their respective departments; and he made this clear at new employee orientations. Allen called these orientations "The Lund Way." There, Allen would try to imbue employees with two central tenets of ALC culture. The first tenet was honesty, always conducting business the right way no matter the cost. The second tenet was self-sufficiency. If your team could build a system or find a solution, that was preferred to outsourcing the tasks to third party vendors. A commitment to self-sufficiency encouraged employees to challenge themselves to find creative approaches. It particularly required the support departments to expand in personnel and capability; and it made Allen Lund Company the multi-faceted business powerhouse it is today.

ALC has large-company-capability with small-company-culture, an accomplishment only achieved by a third tenet that isn't spelled out in "The Lund Way" Orientation, but was embodied by Allen during his life. Caring about people was not a theoretical or even passive notion. Allen made sure his employees *felt* cared about. Despite the commitment to self-sufficiency, for Allen there must be no doubt in his employees' minds that they had his support. When he spoke to someone, it was with a special attentiveness that made them feel they were the only person in the room. He checked in on people, not just about the work they were doing but the lives they were living outside the office. When someone in the office asked how he was, Allen would often smile and reply: "It's your world, I'm just living in it." In other words, 'It's not about me. I'm here to help you, however I can. If you're good, I'm good.'

After Kenny was promoted to Vice President, Allen would promote Chetan Tandon to be ALC's Chief Information Officer. Chetan was born in India and came to the United States for college on a student visa. He was hired by a consulting firm right after graduation. One of the firm's clients was Allen Lund Company. Kenny, who was still managing the IT department at the time, saw Chetan's talent and hired him in 2000. Allen agreed to sponsor Chetan when he applied for his green card. Although obtaining his green card would mean Chetan would no longer be contractually obligated to stay at the same company, the environment Allen had created at ALC was one he wouldn't want to leave.

In 2002, the ALC IT department launched Oracle Financials as their new financial system. It went live early one morning and Chetan had stayed in the office the night before to make sure everything went smoothly. Allen, who usually arrived at work around 5:00 a.m., found Chetan sleeping on a couch. The launch was an enormous undertaking and had been the focus of the entire IT department for months. However, Allen's first question to Chetan in the morning wasn't about how it went or how the system was working. Allen asked if he could buy him breakfast or run to grab him coffee. He asked how Chetan was personally. Allen of course had an enormous interest in how the launch went, but people always came first.

The story stuck with Chetan through the years as it embodied Allen's style of leadership and it served as proof he had chosen the right company in which to spend his career. After working towards the goal for seventeen years, Chetan finally obtained his US citizenship and couldn't wait to share the news with Allen. Allen was extremely patriotic, often closing manager meetings by singing "God Bless America." Allen felt his own life was proof of the American Dream, and he carried a deep gratitude for his country. When Allen saw Chetan's new passport, he was overjoyed and sent out an email to every ALC office around the country asking them to celebrate this achievement. The offices decorated their spaces with red, white, and blue streamers and balloons. It was a company-wide "Happy Citizenship Day!" The offices sent cards and photos of their celebrations and Allen compiled a collage of them for Chetan. Allen also gave Chetan the cherished American Flag he kept on his desk; a symbol of just how proud Allen was of his employee.

Allen knew that if you treat an employee well, they will want to stick around. He also remembered how difficult his early days were at Foss Lewis, living paycheck to paycheck. He had wrestled with a lot of uncertainty about the possibility of something happening to him that would leave Kathie alone with young children and no protection. So Allen Lund Company put together an extensive employee benefit package. Providing his employees and their families with the best health care possible was one of the benefits about which Allen and Kathie were most proud. They vowed that no matter what was happening with the company or the economy, they would remain aggressive in providing benefits to their employees.

When Hurricane Harvey hit Houston TX in 2017, the ALC office in Houston had just opened. Their office space on the second floor was okay, but the lobby of the building flooded, forcing them to work out of an employee's home. Allen called them to check in. The new manager explained they were going to have to let an employee go because there weren't enough loads in the area to justify the additional person they just hired. The storm had thrown a wrench in the manager's plan to be profitable within the first six months. Allen told him not to worry about profit at the moment. The corporate office would provide additional support and profitability would come eventually. Allen then asked if they had already signed a contract with this new employee, which they had. He encouraged them to honor the contract. Allen knew that if you honor your employees they will, in turn, honor you.

Allen's deep commitment to the people who worked for him resulted in many of them staying with the company for the duration of their careers. To date, Allen Lund Company has over two hundred employees who have been with the company for over ten years, and over a third of them have been there over twenty years. A few of the company's charter members are still working at ALC to this day.

Allen always seemed to see opportunities where other people saw challenges. During the 2001 recession, he wrote a letter to his company declaring they would not be participating in the recession. He had every manager sign it as if it were the Declaration of Independence, and a copy went out to each office to be placed on display. As simple as it was, it caused everyone in the company to stop speaking about the recession. No excuses were made. No gripes were heard. They were challenged to go out and find new loads.

As the economy reeled, Allen also saw an opportunity to harvest talent from other companies who were retrenching. ALC seized the opportunity to bring in talented new people. At the end of 2001, the company's workforce had grown and revenue was up by twenty percent.

In another instance, several companies who Allen did business with filed for bankruptcy. They all owed Allen Lund Company a substantial amount of money, which they now would not have to pay. It was a major blow to the company, but Allen saw it as an opportunity to improve their policies and empower his employees.

For example, they would need to strengthen their company credit policy. Allen came up with a plan, but decided he wanted to open the discussion to the managers, explaining how recent events were going to affect the company. The managers came up with a policy that was stricter than Allen's original draft, but one with which they felt comfortable. Allen listened to his managers and felt he was accountable to them, especially where finances were concerned. The managers' new policy was implemented.

There is a Biblical principle Jesus taught his disciples: The last shall be first, and the first shall be last. In the Gospel of Matthew Jesus says, "Those who are greatest among you, should take the lowest rank, and the leader should be like a servant." Allen wanted to embody this teaching in his heart-posture toward all ALC employees. They may have been his employees, but Allen felt as if he was working for them. ALC's success meant the company could benefit more families. Allen believed the business world had a powerful capacity to positively impact lives and communities because he understood just how much dignity having a solid job could give someone. Providing a good job was a chance to change a life.

Allen sat on the Board of Directors for an organization called Homeboy Industries, a youth program whose mission is to assist high risk youth, former gang members, and recently incarcerated individuals to build better lives. They offer counseling, tattoo removal, job training, and a variety of other services with the ultimate goal of helping them find employment. Homeboy Industries was started by Father Greg Boyle, a Jesuit priest serving at Dolores Mission Church in the Boyle Heights neighborhood of Los Angeles.

In 2001, Father Boyle approached Allen about hiring someone who had formerly been incarcerated. Giving someone a second chance would be a greater gift than any financial contribution. Father Boyle told Allen about a man named Phillip Amador. Phillip grew up on the streets of Boyle Heights and spent his youth oscillating between a juvenile detention center and a youth program at Father Boyle's parish. He was a member of Al Capone, a gang that trafficked narcotics and constantly warred with surrounding rival gangs. He survived several shootouts and often did some of the shooting. He did many horrible things under the Al Capone banner. After he was convicted of a third felony, the judge sentenced him to life in prison. Due to a technical flaw found in a witness' statement, Phillip was released from prison after serving five years.

While he was still incarcerated, Phillip's younger brother was recruited into a gang, which didn't sit right with him as a protective older brother. Tragically, his brother caught a bullet to the neck during a shootout. The bullet only grazed his carotid artery, but it hit his cervical vertebrae. He survived, but it left him quadriplegic, wheelchair bound for the rest of his life.

The news of his brother's injury broke Phillip's heart. He was finally ready to go to Father Boyle and find a new path for his life. Father Boyle welcomed him at Homeboy Industries. The City of Los Angeles had given them funding to pay participants to remove graffiti from buildings around the neighborhood. Phillip began working for Father Boyle and even had the gang tattoos on his head and forearms removed, an outward expression of his new beginning. Philip was now taking care of his wife and his brother, so Father Boyle was eager to find him a better employment opportunity.

Allen needed to consider this proposition carefully. He believed everyone deserved a second chance, but he also wanted to ensure other employees would be comfortable with the idea. He sought the counsel of his sons and several managers. He was candid with them about Phillip's story. If the company did this, they would need to find the right opportunity for Phillip, and the manager of that department would need to approve. The manager of marketing was eager to help. She started Phillip in data entry.

The corporate world intimidated Phillip more than anything he had seen on the streets. He was awestruck pulling his car up to the office on his first day. He never imagined he would ever work in a place like this. Phillip confided his nervous thoughts to Allen, who told him not to worry. They were going to make sure he succeeded; and they did. When Phillip began data entry, he was typing on the keyboard with one finger.

Allen paid for him to take a typing class at a local community college in Montrose. Allen checked on Phillip every day to see how he was faring. Phillip had to learn an entirely new way of communicating in the professional corporate world. Allen was there to help and encourage him. Phillip was promoted into the carrier compliance department and from there was promoted again to work on accounts payable and accounts receivable.

Allen sought to give Phillip every opportunity to learn and grow within the company. He sent Phillip and his family to their office in Texas so he could work as a broker. Even with Allen's help, Phillip initially struggled to settle into the corporate ecosystem. He needed to learn new problem-solving skills. His greatest struggle continued to be feeling like a fish-out-of-water. On several occasions, Phillip wanted to give up. He felt demotivated by the fact that he didn't fit in, to which Allen told him, "If you don't strive for the best, you won't get the best. You don't give up in this life, you have to keep going. You have to keep fighting the good fight in order to reap the rewards on the other side."

Phillip now works in the customer service department at the ALC corporate office. He is a part of the team that manages one of ALC's largest accounts: Costco. On average, Phillip's department handles approximately two thousand emails per day. He types his replies with the skills Allen helped Phillip obtain. His life has been forever changed. He has been married for twenty years. He is a father of four, a proud grandfather to two baby girls, and an employee of Allen Lund Company for twenty-three years and counting. Two years into working with ALC, Phillip was named "Homeboy of the Year" and gave a speech upon receiving his award. He credited Allen with helping to change his life. For Allen, that was what the business was all about—to do as much good as possible.

In 2009, Allen decided to participate in a corporate work-study program, partnering with Verbum Dei High School. The program offered paid internships to students who worked for the company one or two days per week. Allen wanted to give students, who wouldn't otherwise have the opportunity, a chance to learn the skills necessary to get a job in corporate America. The students worked on rotation with other students in their class who share the same job with them. They were given a chance to work for various departments to get exposure to different types of jobs. Though there was a mentoring aspect to the program, they were ultimately treated like any other employee, with expectations and responsibilities. Allen realized many of these students had experienced a tough part of life, and believed they could rise above it to become model citizens: talented, well educated, and hardworking. To date, Allen Lund Company continues its partnership with Verbum Dei.

Allen was committed to doing as much good as he could for as many people as he could. His company was one of the

Allen, age 3, with his mom, Maxine, and dog Tippie.

Allen enlists in the Army Reserve after graduating high school in 1958.

Allen and Kathie on their wedding day, July 16, 1960, at St. Joseph's Catholic Church in Ogden, UT.

Allen and Kathie with David, Natalie, and Kenny in 1965.

Family picture taken in 1975 for the Incarnation Catholic Church Parish Directory in Glendale.

First Official Board of Directors meeting for the Allen Lund Company in 1996. Front Row: Kenny, Christina, Terry Walker, Kathie, Anna, Natalie, Steve Asip, Eddie, and Dennis Connors. Back Row: David, Joe Hillman and Allen.

Allen Lund Company Corporate employees celebrate reaching 100 million in sales in 1998.

The family leaders of the Allen Lund Company in 2015.

Allen and Kathie celebrating with the Carmelite Sisters of the Most Sacred Heart of Los Angeles.

University of Portland dedication of Lund Family Hall. Allen and Kathie are presented with a portrait of the hall by Fr. Mark Poorman.

Allen surrounded by his grandchildren at the dedication mass of Lund Family Hall at the University of Portland.

Kenny, David, Eddie, Allen and Kirk in front of the original
Long Canyon Ranch cabin on their annual hunting trip.

Allen in his element at Long Canyon Ranch, taking his
grandsons for a ride on the excavator.

Lund Family picture in 2014.

Photos by Bronson Photography (www.bronsonphotography.com)

Allen and his grandkids on Halloween. Trick-or-treating at his office was a yearly tradition!

Allen with his angels, otherwise known as his granddaughters on Grandparent's Day in 2014 at Flintridge Sacred Heart Academy.

Allen playing Santa Claus and handing out presents to the grandkids at Long Canyon Ranch in 2014.

Allen and Kathie in Israel alongside the Sea of Galilee where Kathie would later revisit after Allen's passing.

Praying over Allen at mass celebrated by Fr. Matt Elshoff during Allen's final days, or as we fondly refer to his "finest" hour.

resources he used to accomplish that. He constantly strived to provide opportunities for people to make something of their lives and experience meaningful careers. The enormous amounts of hard work that went into building ALC from the ground up was like a spark that spread like a wildfire. It changed the lives of his family. It changed the lives of their families. It changed the lives of his employees, and many more people to come.

CHAPTER FIFTEEN

MINISTRY OF PRESENCE

"By the grace God has given me, I laid a foundation as a wise builder, and someone else is building on it. But each should build with care."

—*Apostle Paul, 1 Corinthians 3:10*

In 2003, Allen and Kathie moved to a new house in Pasadena, which Allen remodeled and added a library for himself near the front entrance. It was a small room, only designed to fit a few people comfortably, but it was a perfect place for Allen to nestle into his armchair, read a book, or watch a show on TV. The channel was usually on shows like *Ice Road Truckers* or *Deadliest Catch*. There was a comical reality to this cozy library. Everyone in the family always wanted to be wherever Allen was, so they would forgo sitting in the larger living room and hang out with Allen instead. This meant the tiny sitting room was often overcrowded with family members and friends. If Allen would have known this would happen, he would have designed it to be a much larger space. Nevertheless, he loved the company.

With six children, Allen and Kathie's home always appeared to have a revolving door of guests. When the Lund kids invited friends over, they would always come straight into the library to say hello to Mr. Lund before doing anything else. As they grew up, the Lund children never went through the stage many young people do where they are embarrassed by their parents. On the contrary, they wanted everyone to meet their Mom and Dad. Allen loved getting to know his children's friends. He'd ask how they were doing in school, sports, etc, wanting to make sure they were on a good path. Allen treated them like he did his own kids and many of these friends became so intertwined with the Lund family that they felt they'd somehow been unofficially adopted.

As the children were growing up, Allen was only strict about a handful of things. One of them was curfew. While Eddie was still in high school, he and his friend Michael Betance decided to try to talk Allen into extending the curfew to give them an extra half hour. Eventually, Michael, not Eddie, became the one to work up the courage to ask "Mr. Lund." Whenever anyone asked Allen for anything, they had to put together a strong argument. They needed to be prepared for Allen's inevitable follow-up questions. Eddie played football, basketball, and baseball in high school and Allen loved attending all his games and even served on the Booster Club (a group of fathers who supported the athletic department). Michael played all the same sports as Eddie. Michael was a good kid, a great athlete, and a competent curfew negotiator because Allen agreed to the extra half hour.

Allen also admired Michael's family. The Betances were a tight-knit, hard-working family. Michael's father was a general manager at a carwash and provided for eight children. Allen had a deep respect for him. The Betances lived far from St. Francis, so during football season Michael spent game nights sleeping at the Lunds' house. One day, Allen was asking Michael about his college plans. Eddie had decided to attend Notre Dame, but Michael was still unsure of what life would look like after high school graduation. He told Mr. Lund that he would also love to attend Notre Dame, but hadn't applied because his family didn't have the money to afford college tuition; especially tuition at a private college like that one. Allen told him to apply anyway. He didn't want money to be the reason Michael didn't apply for something he wanted. Allen offered to pay Michael's tuition if he got in and genuinely had his heart set on going.

Michael knew Mr. Lund meant every word of the offer. Allen was always generous, but as he became more successful, he was able to help people on a larger scale. His generosity, however, was balanced with discernment. Although Allen had the means to write checks and make things happen, he knew this was not the most meaningful way he could have an impact on the lives of the people around him. Just like he enjoyed rolling up his sleeves, hopping on a machine, and doing a project, he also wanted to be actively involved in the projects he chose to help with and the people he chose to mentor. The greatest gift Allen often gave people was his presence. He'd give gentle and wise advice to nudge people in directions he could see them flourishing.

Allen's next words to Michael would change the direction of his life. Allen told Michael he should also consider applying for one of the military academies. He felt it could be good for Michael and his family. Allen even offered to help him secure a nomination letter.

In order to apply for one of the academies a candidate needed a letter from a congressman. Allen's time working with the Transportation Intermediaries of America gave him contacts in Washington D.C. David Dreier, a congressman from Ventura County, CA would frequently call Allen with questions about legislation concerning the transportation industry. Allen was confident he could call in a favor if Michael needed it. The academies are prestigious and excellent educational institutions. There is no tuition to attend. Instead, admitted students must commit to time in the military after graduation. Michael listened intently as Mr. Lund explained how he would hire a graduate from any of the military academies because attendance there speaks highly of an individual.

Michael took Allen's advice that day and went on to attend

the United States Air Force Academy. After graduation, he served his commitment with the Air Force during the Clinton Administration. He first attended pilot training, but demand for pilots at the time was low. He was banked, and returned to the Academy to coach football for the remainder of his military commitment. While working as a coach, he earned his MBA from a college in Colorado Springs.

After his military career, Michael asked Allen for a loan to start his own construction business. Allen listened to his pitch, but declined. He instead offered to coach Michael through the process of securing a loan from a bank. Allen said if he was unsuccessful there, then he would help him financially. But securing a bank loan was a part of the business Michael would need to learn in order to be successful moving forward.

Allen became a business mentor to Michael, which was more powerful than simply being an investor. Although Allen didn't give Michael the initial loan, Allen cosigned on a line of credit. He also eventually helped Michael financially during a rough patch in his business. Allen never told anyone. When Allen chose to help someone, he tried to do it quietly and strategically. He often wanted his giving to be anonymous. Allen wanted to make sure his giving never stunted anyone's personal growth. Hard work and problem solving can help shape a person for long lasting success. So Allen was discerning about the type of help he offered and when he offered it. He would look for people who had initiative and try to find the best way to come alongside them to get them started on a good path.

Michael wasn't the only friend of the family Allen took under his wing. Michael's brother ended up working for Allen Lund Company for twenty-eight years. There were many other people Allen mentored, including Kathleen Hurley (Dick Hurley's daughter) who was a neighbor on Isabel Street. She became like an instant daughter to Allen the moment she stepped on a bee in their front yard. Allen consoled the crying five-year-old and pulled out the stinger. Kathleen spent a lot of her time at the Lunds' house growing up. Now, two generations of Lunds and Hurleys had become close friends. Allen was Kathleen's softball coach at Flintridge Sacred Heart Academy. He teased her, often saying if he died and could come back as anyone he would want her life because she had it so good. Poking fun was one of Allen's love languages and Kathleen could give the sass right back to him.

When Kathleen met and married her husband, Mark Snashall, Allen's lighthearted teasing transferred over to him. Mark was from England and Allen initiated him into American culture through a series of ongoing pranks. These rituals would become increasingly creative over time. Mark was a huge Chelsea Football Club fan. He named his company Chelsea Construction after the team and even bought a blue truck to reflect the team's color. The team's rival is the Arsenal Football Club. Knowing this, Allen and David took Mark's truck, had it spray-painted Arsenal red, and added a bunch of their team stickers to the bumper. Mark was flabbergasted but impressed when he came out of work and saw the vehicle.

Mark loved to prank the Lunds in retaliation. When Allen and Kathie were planning Christina's wedding Mark called Christina, disguised his accent, and pretended to be the church informing them they would need to change the date of the wedding due to a scheduling conflict. This caused her to panic since invitations had already been sent and the wedding was only a few months away. Allen heard about the call after work, was very upset, and drove to the church the following morning to confront the priest. The confused priest finally looked at Allen and told him it was the first day of April and more than likely someone had pranked him for April Fools Day.

Kenny and Allen planned a comeback so epic it made local news. They had an enormous banner made that read: "Hooters— Opening Soon! Applicants Call This Number…" They included Mark's phone number on the sign and posted it on a local construction site in La Canada, a very conservative town. Mark was in London visiting his family when the calls started. When he got home he realized what had happened because his voicemail was littered with a hysterical combination of concerned city council members launching their complaints and young women looking for a job.

All jokes aside, Allen became a mentor and friend to Mark. The two spent many Sundays together, often attending the 6:30 a.m. Mass, grabbing breakfast, and hunting for new gadgets at a local swap meet. Allen was also the one who initially encouraged Mark to start his own business. Allen rented office space to Mark at the ALC Building and also shared his machinery expertise with Mark, going with him to purchase his first truck and first Bobcat. Allen would do anything to make sure Kathleen and Mark were on a good path. He continued to champion them as years went by. The couple became so close to the Lunds that even their six children became like family to Allen.

Many people throughout the years felt that way with Allen. He loved deeply and welcomed many into his home. Fatherhood was a calling he lived out in various ways, and Kathie was his match as a nurturing matriarch to many people. As their kids started families, Allen and Kathie wholeheartedly embraced the joys of being grandparents. They showed up at as many plays, games, and events as possible, determined to cheer their grandchildren on in every endeavor. Allen loved to prank the grandkids. He teased them, loved them, listened to them, and made them feel they were the most important people in the room. The grandchildren would also bring their friends over to their grandparents house, and they too would stop in the library to say hello to "Mr. Lund" before they did anything else.

There were many perks to being a Lund grandchild. For

Allen, they were his top priority. If they came to his office, he always made time to see them. Business calls could wait. St. Francis High School hosts a 6:45 a.m. Mass for the community every morning. Allen attended Mass daily and was pleased when his family attended as well. On one occasion, Katherine Lund, Allen's granddaughter, called him at the office. She and her sisters and cousin had also attended the early Mass before school. They realized, however, when they arrived at Flintridge Sacred Heart that they'd gotten their class schedules confused and had several hours before class started. Her first thought was to ask her grandfather if he wanted to go with them to breakfast. Allen dropped everything he was doing, got in his truck, and met them at the restaurant. Even though it was a busy day at the office, he made time for them. Allen would never miss an opportunity to have a breakfast like this one.

His twenty-two grandchildren followed in their parents' footsteps, with the boys attending St. Francis and the girls attending Flintridge Sacred Heart Academy. However, there was a time when the future of St. Francis High School was uncertain. After his sons had graduated, Allen heard the school wasn't doing well financially and enrollment was dwindling. Allen was motivated to step in and help.

Although Allen could have written a check to help the institution, he knew that short-term solutions could not create long-lasting results. St. Francis didn't get into its financial struggles overnight. For Allen to truly help, he would need to first assess what was and wasn't working at the school.

In 1991, Allen put together a committee of parents of St. Francis alumni. Members of this illustrious team included business owners and captains of industry. Their first task was to evaluate the school's spending and eliminate unnecessary expenditures. Allen was extremely meticulous when looking over the books. His pragmatic instincts told him he would need to first stabilize the institution before the real work of rebuilding it could begin.

There were many parallels between how Allen ran his company and how he approached external projects like this one. Allen always waited for the right people to be put in place before he expanded his company into any new territories. He also believed wholeheartedly that leadership trickled down. If he wanted the company culture to be right, it needed to start with who he placed in charge. His approach to St. Francis was no different. Allen was selective about the members he included on the committee; a team that would one day operate in an official capacity as the school's Board of Directors. Allen also felt strongly that the role of the principal should be solely focused on ensuring academic and administrative excellence. Up until this point, the role of a St. Francis principal was too multi-faceted. In addition to running the school, the principal was also responsible for fundraising to keep the institution afloat. Allen decided dividing the responsibilities between two positions would allow for specialization and greater success. He felt a school president should be appointed and Father Matt Elshoff was the perfect man for the job.

Father Matt had been connected to the school as a student and as a member of the faculty. He graduated from St. Francis High School in 1973 and went on to earn a master's degree from Graduate Theological Union in Berkeley, California. He joined the Capuchin Franciscan Order and after his ordination in 1982 he was assigned to St. Francis High School as the vocational director of the province of Our Lady of Angels. In 1985 he returned to St. Francis High School to teach and serve as the admissions director and campus minister. Father Matt served in this capacity from 1985 to 1989. This is where he met Allen. Everyone at St. Francis High School respected Father Matt. His passion, focus, and energy made him the ideal candidate. Allen also felt it was important that the school maintain its Franciscan culture by always keeping a Franciscan presence at the leadership table. Allen convinced Father Matt, who was now working at the Capuchin Franciscan Novitiate, San Lorenzo Seminary in Santa Ynez, California to return to St. Francis High School as its president. Allen explained that Father Matt would be in charge of all of the spiritual and financial needs of the school. He also asked Father Matt to accompany him on a thirty-three-mile drive to West Hills, California to convince another former teacher to return to St. Francis.

Tom Moran was an English teacher and baseball coach at St. Francis from 1975 until 1990. All three of Allen's sons were in his classes and Tom had the reputation for being one of the toughest teachers at the school. It was nearly impossible to get an "A" in his class. Despite his reputation for being tough, however, he was deeply respected by students. Tom was a hard worker and poured an exceeding amount of love and devotion into his classroom. Allen believed that if anyone could steward the academic excellence of St. Francis, it was Tom.

Tom had left the school for the opportunity to be the principal at Chaminade High School. It was the right next step for his career, but just before he was to renew his contract with Chaminade in 1993, Allen and Father Matt came to talk him into returning to St. Francis High School. Tom was surprised by the offer to be principal of St. Francis. That role was always filled by a priest, and Tom would be the first layperson to take up the mantle.

Allen made a compelling argument for why Tom should return and Allen shared his vision for carrying St. Francis forward. But Tom didn't need much convincing. He knew Allen and had seen his integrity and work ethic over the years. It was clear that he would have Allen's full support if he decided to come back, and Allen's support was like having jet fuel in your engine.

Tom agreed to return to St. Francis. With proper leadership in place, Allen and the board could begin the work of rebuilding the school. Throughout this process, Allen consistently prioritized long-term sustainability over short-term success. They should rebuild the right way and should never compromise on the vision of turning St. Francis into a premier school that equips students with the best educational and spiritual training possible.

In response to St. Francis' poor enrollment, a short-term solution many people would have chosen would have been to reduce admissions standards to fill the seats. However, Tom suggested they take the opposite approach. When Allen placed someone in a position, he listened to them and trusted them to make decisions. Tom felt strongly that admission to St. Francis needed to be a meaningful achievement. He wanted to raise the standards for enrollment, believing it would eventually raise the caliber of students and increase the overall academic standard of the school.

Allen understood that raising the criteria for admission and therefore turning some previously eligible students away would cause numbers to initially dip. However, Allen and Father Matt shared Tom's vision. So they were willing to sacrifice short-term gains for long-term results.

Allen instead turned his attention to renovating the campus. Upgrading classrooms, improving facilities, and equipping students with state-of-the-art tools would attract attention to the school and bolster enrollment. Real estate in La Canada is an expensive and competitive venture. Due to where St. Francis was logistically and financially, all new facilities would need to be built within the existing property lines already owned by the school. It was decided the first building project the board would tackle was a large parking structure. Plans were drawn up and a capital campaign was launched.

No one was more excited about construction than Allen. He drove by the school every day to look at the progress. He also consistently called his family members to update them on the progress. He was excited, proud, and gave the parking garage the same level of attention as most people would give a symphony hall. Even in a building as utilitarian as this, Allen felt it needed to be beautiful and it needed to be excellent. Not only was that aim accomplished, but the project also finished on time and within budget.

Every single renovation or building project came within or under budget. To Allen, staying within a budget was the same as keeping his word. The board gained a reputation for efficiency which helped them continue fundraising efforts. After the completion of the parking structure, the board could focus on other projects. Allen never wanted the board to overextend itself so they took construction projects on one at a time. There was a debate for the board about what to do next. There were two major construction projects on the table: a new athletic training center and renovated field and a new theatre on campus.

A meeting was scheduled to discuss the proposals and representatives from the theatre and athletic departments attended to make their presentations. Everyone expected Allen to rally behind the athletic department. He had been Booster Club President and still attended sports games at St. Francis. However, at the top of the meeting before any presentations were made, Allen surprised everyone. He said that it was clear to him which project needed to be done first, and that was building a theatre. The school already had a building for the athletic department, and Allen had the foresight to know raising money for that project would be easier than most and could therefore happen later. The school however didn't have a theatre at all. The theatre department had been renting out spaces off campus to host their concerts and productions. Allen felt St. Francis was known for its academics and athletics, but to provide a well-rounded education for the students, it needed to invest in the arts as well.

No one in that board room was more shocked to hear this statement from Allen's lips than Emmanuel "Manny" Eulalia, the theatre teacher who sat in the corner holding the pages of his prepared petition. He never gave his presentation to the board because they unanimously followed Allen's lead. Conversations instead focused on what this project would entail.

Allen had a natural talent for communicating things simply

and confidently. He spoke in a way that made people listen. He also had the unique skill of confidently fitting in wherever he was. He was comfortable whether he was sitting in a boardroom chair, in a church pew, or on the back of a tractor. Few people had that kind of social dexterity. However, Allen never did boast about it. Instead, he approached every project with a great deal of humility. He believed he needed to rely on the expertise of others to tell him what they needed to have a successful and functional campus. Allen talked to everyone at the school to get their opinions on projects. He consulted with the faculty, administrators, and custodians, taking all of their feedback under advisement. He also raised their salaries on average by 20 percent, moving away from the original Archdiocesan pay-scale in favor of performance based pay raises, demonstrating he wasn't just interested in building buildings. He ultimately wanted to build up people.

When drawing up plans for the theatre, Allen listened to and supported Manny Eulalia's vision for his department. Manny wanted a real theatre where students could create high caliber productions. The short list for a building like this included adequate stage space, wings, a fly system, professional lighting mounts, and an orchestra pit. Allen agreed that if something was worth doing, it was worth doing right. He didn't know anything about building a theatre but Allen listened to Manny and committed to researching the minutiae of the project. Just as he did with the parking structure, Allen was so excited about every detail of the space, down to the special air conditioning unit they installed in the theatre that would quietly keep temperatures perfect for audiences attending their productions.

The theatre department grew exponentially after this investment. They now put on two major productions per year with sold out shows that run for more than two weeks of performances. Live orchestras accompany the students and professionals in the industry, musicians, and production designers volunteer their time to help students gain competitive industry experience. Allen and the Board of Directors also raised money to update the department's film and television studio, provisioning them with excellent equipment, studio space, and editing bays. Students interested in TV and film work to create news segments and human interest pieces for the school's live broadcasts. They learn to write, produce, announce, film, and edit for television. Students in the program have gone on to attend prestigious arts colleges, win Emmys, and achieve long-term success in the film and television industry.

Allen was extremely proud of the department and what the board was able to build for the student experience. He often gave tours of the space to friends on the weekends. His enthusiasm for the projects organically turned friends into investors, and the theatre department became as well funded as the athletic department, making St. Francis High School a triple threat of academic, athletic, and artistic education.

After the theatre was finished on time and within budget, Allen turned his attention to the launch of capital campaigns for a new athletic training center and updated turf field. The turf for the field was shipped from one of Allen's customers in Georgia on ALC trucks. The Board also raised money for a new entrance to the school, an updated chapel, and classroom renovations. Allen employed the same attention to detail, humility, and dedication to every ambition. The efforts not only gave the school a face lift and increased enrollment; it also opened up greater opportunities for students to receive the best education possible.

The Board at St. Francis was happy to have Allen leading the charge. For nineteen years, he poured heart and soul into making a difference there, an impact that was much deeper than simply making a donation. Allen had such a presence at St. Francis. His fingerprints could be found all over the campus, but one would be hard-pressed to find his name etched on any of the walls. Though the school offered to name a building after him, Allen never wanted that. Allen's joy came from attending events at the school and seeing the places he worked so hard to build getting used by students. He loved attending games and even started to attend all of the theatre department's productions. This was a new experience for Allen, who in the past had rarely attended shows or even movies in theatres. After the shows at St. Francis, he would throw an arm around Manny, congratulate him, and the two men would cry together tears of gratitude for what started as a pile of brick and mortar had become a haven for young people to grow.

CHAPTER SIXTEEN
THERE WITH BELLS ON

"We shall always place education side by side with instruction; the mind will not be cultivated at the expense of the heart. While we prepare useful citizens for society, we shall likewise do our utmost to prepare citizens for heaven."

—Bl. Basil Moreau

In the early days of their marriage, Allen and Kathie had sacrificed a lot to send their children to private Catholic schools. They agreed it was a worthy financial investment to pour into their children's lives. In Utah, Allen felt it was important for his children to attend Catholic schools to give them a sense of community since most of their neighbors belonged to a different faith tradition. As his children continued in school, Allen became even more persuaded of the merits of Catholic education, so he and Kathie made sure to enroll their children in Catholic schools when they moved to California.

Allen felt a life centered on the teachings of Christ was a firm foundation on which to build, and that good education trained the heart as well as the mind. For this reason, Allen wanted to see institutions like St. Francis High School maintain their strength. Although they broke ground on many building projects during his nineteen year tenure as chairman of the board, Allen felt all of that work rested on the surface of a much deeper mission.

Part of Allen's goal for the restoration of St. Francis was to re-enforce the school's commitment to Franciscan culture. The school was named after St. Francis of Assisi, who lived in Italy during the thirteenth century and founded the Franciscan Order of the Catholic Church. St. Francis endeavored to live a life focused on the Gospel, and he put particular emphasis on the denial of self and Scripture's charge to take up one's cross daily to follow Christ.

There was an expression that circulated around the school which insinuated that Franciscan culture was "more caught than taught." In other words, the school had always been led by Franciscan priests and their presence would undoubtedly leave an impression on students in attendance. However, Allen and the leadership at the school felt strongly that there needed to be greater intentionality in their mission to imbue students with Franciscan ideas and practices. This conviction motivated many of Allen's initiatives as chair.

Allen requested board meetings be opened and closed with prayer. Every class at the school started with a prayer as well.

The faculty were given packets containing Scripture and prayers they could say with students each day. It wasn't a mandate, but rather a starting point for fostering spiritual growth among the teachers. The purpose was to equip the faculty with more spiritual resources and tools to bring prayer more effortlessly into the classrooms.

At the same time, the school began an initiative to incorporate sixteen Franciscan virtues into the curriculum. These virtues were: prayer, compassion, simplicity, gratitude, integrity, humility, brotherhood, joy, acceptance, service, generosity, peacemaking, faithfulness, hospitality, charity, and goodness. Every quarter, the school focused on one of the virtues which meant that after four years of high school every student learned about all sixteen. These ethics were woven into the curriculum and into the selected prayers of each classroom.

Allen felt it was important that students and faculty had the opportunity to learn about the spiritual roots of Franciscan life, so the board sponsored a yearly pilgrimage to Assisi, Italy. Students had the opportunity to apply to go on the trip, and every year the school paid for several faculty and staff members to go as well. The itinerary included a visit to the Basilica of St. Francis of Assisi, which was built in 1228 AD and is the burial site of the saint. This spiritual retreat was a treasured experience for faculty members and students who found the excursion restorative and inspirational.

These are a few examples of the measures Allen supported to fortify the spiritual identity of the school. However, every decision, big or small, was evaluated based on how it fit into the central mission. Allen believed in the power of having a mission statement, which is why he developed one for his own company. It provided vital clarity and a united vision for moving forward. He felt once an institution's mission was established, there should be no deviation. The role of a Catholic school was to teach students about Christ and educate them with excellence. Every decision was weighed with how well it accomplished that commission.

Many of the Lund children continued their Catholic educations into their collegiate years. Christina, the youngest, was a student at the University of Portland. During her year studying abroad in Europe, Allen and Kathie flew out to visit. Over a night of playing cards in the student lounge, Allen made friends with the Holy Cross priests who were overseeing the trip. Making friends in general was Allen's modus operandi, but he had a unique talent for connecting with clergy. Whereas most people are reserved and feel as if they must be on their best behavior when speaking to a person of the cloth, Allen was the same no matter the company he kept. A mixture of personal integrity and being comfortable in his own skin meant Allen was as at ease talking to a priest as he was chatting with one of his hunting buddies. This is not to say Allen didn't have reverence for members of the clergy. As a devout parishioner, Allen respected the leadership and service that members gave to their flocks. Allen simply wasn't self-conscious. He never attempted to impress anyone. His focus was to make sure other people were comfortable and this down-to-earth humility put the priests at ease. They too could be fully themselves around Allen and Kathie.

After the trip they asked Allen to join a business advisory committee at the University of Portland, which humbled and honored Allen. He fell in love with the Congregation of the Holy Cross, a family of priests focused on preaching the Gospel and educating youth. Holy Cross universities emphasize the importance of pastoral care for students. Every dormitory contains its own chapel and has a priest in residence, one of many spiritual resources made available to students during their time on campus. The Holy Cross mission resonated with Allen who would later be asked to join the Board of Regents and eventually be asked to become Chair.

This honor always humbled Allen because he had never attended college, and part of the reason he worked so hard was so his children could have that opportunity. Although he didn't come from the world of academia, representatives from the school felt he had a wonderful grasp on the university's needs. His sharp business mind, ability to see the big picture, and straight-forward communication style were assets as the board put together a ten-year-plan to improve the campus.

The University of Portland sits on a bluff, overlooking the Willamette River and downtown Portland. Allen and Kathie wanted to donate something significant to the school. They proposed a prayer walk be added to campus along the cliffside, but the university had a bigger idea for the first project on the docket. They expressed to the board a desire for the University of Portland to have an iconic symbol that elevated the school grounds; a symbol by which the University would be recognized. They proposed a Bell Tower be added to the heart of campus, and Allen and the board began plans right away. The 95-foot tower would be the tallest structure on campus, house fourteen bells, and be adorned by a brushed steel cross with the Latin words "Ave Crux Spes Unica," which translates to "Hail to the Cross, Our One Hope." Construction began in 2008, a 1.3 million dollar endeavor predominantly funded by the donations of Allen and Kathie along with a few other donors, many of whom were Allen and Kathie's personal friends.

Like all building projects Allen oversaw, he would constantly call to get updates on the progress of construction. Allen called Jim Lyons, Vice President of University Relations, each day to talk about the bell tower. Allen's meticulous and curious mind was interested in every single detail of the design. The university eventually installed a webcam for Allen so he could watch the progress from southern California. Allen and Kathie flew out to Amsterdam to a traditional bell foundry for the casting of the new bells. They'd involved their friends in the project, encouraging them to donate a bell and come with them to watch them being made. The benefactors were able to add things they brought from home to be melted down into the bronze during the casting process. The bells ranged in weight from 77 to 1,400 pounds.

Construction of the belltower was completed in 2009. Father Bill Beauchamp, President of the University at the time, remarked that the tower served as a visual reminder of the university's core commitment to faith in Christ. The chiming of the bells on campus did more than simply remind students of the time. It created a tranquil and reverential atmosphere across the grounds like an unofficial call to prayer or constant reminder to acknowledge God throughout the day. The bells also play various hymns for weddings and commencement ceremonies. New students at the university now gather around the belltower for their freshman orientation ceremony, a tradition in which seven of Allen's grandchildren would take part. Allen was enormously proud to see his children and grandchildren attend college. He believed in higher education, but beyond simply obtaining a degree he also wanted them all to have a good collegiate experience.

Allen and Kathie's next major project at the University of Portland was building a new dormitory for students. The new three-story, 82,000 square foot residence hall would have the capacity to house 270 students and staff. Each floor of the hall would include a social lounge for students to gather, study rooms, and washrooms in each wing. Plans for the ground floor of the structure included a chapel, lobby, office, dining concession, and outdoor courtyard. The building would have added amenities like student storage and laundry rooms. Additionally, there were three apartments included in the plans to house full-time hall staff.

Construction began in 2015 and the duration of the project from design to full occupancy happened within a span of just fourteen months. Allen and Kathie's generosity greenlit the project. Together they had committed over ten million dollars to the University of Portland, and as recognition of this the university wanted to name the building after Allen. Their desire to honor him didn't fully align with Allen's humble nature, but eventually he acquiesced to their relentless requests and the name "Lund Family Hall" became the compromise. The name was fitting since several of Allen's family members would live here and enjoy the beautiful space into which Allen and Kathie had poured themselves.

The Lunds were spending a lot more time at the University of Portland, so much so the university gave Allen and Kathie a place on campus for them to stay when visiting. Each dorm on campus had two apartments built into them that were for staff in residence. The room the University of Portland gifted to Allen was in Field's Hall. It had a kitchenette, living room, bedroom, and bath; and Kathie renovated it to create a home away from home. The couple entertained board members, priests, faculty, and family in their apartment when they were there. It was fun for Allen to be able to spend time with his granddaughters, who were students during his tenure as chair.

He'd always bring them to special dinners hosted by the Board of Regents and introduced them to everyone. This wasn't technically allowed, but no one ever told Allen that. The University kept him busy when he was in town, but he always made time for family. When his granddaughter Madelyn needed to buy a car, he snuck off between meetings to take her to the dealership. No one could negotiate a price better than Allen. Madelyn had a set price her parents said she could spend, but Allen added to it and she drove her grandfather back to campus in time for his next meeting in her red Ford Focus.

Allen served as a regent from 2001 to 2007, and was Chair of the Board from 2008 to 2017, making him the longest serving Chair in University of Portland history. During his tenure the university flourished and the campus was completely revitalized. In addition to donating the Bell Tower and Lund Family Hall, Allen and Kathie also contributed to the new Beauchamp Recreation and Wellness Center and gifted to the school a Heritage Illuminated Edition of the Saint John's Bible, which is permanently on display at the Clark Library.

Under his leadership as chair, renovations were also made to the library, business school, engineering school, baseball field, and school cafeteria. In addition to the updates to the physical campus, Allen and Kathie began an endowment fund that provides scholarships for incoming UP freshmen. The University of Portland was forever changed. Allen led with both generosity and wisdom, leaving his mark on the campus. He considered every effort worthwhile because he knew the experiences and lessons the students received during their time there would continue to impact them for the rest of their lives and give them a profound foundation of faith on which to build.

Allen may have never attended college as a student, but he had a collegiate experience more profound than most. He was humbled to walk through campus and encouraged by the progress he saw. The man who often referred to himself as "just a truck driver" never gave formal remarks in one of the lecture halls, but his life was a profound lesson to many leaders at the university. People like Allen and Kathie seem to have a faith so profound it's practically baked into them. For Allen this may have been true, since his commitment to God started in the middle of a Utah wildfire. However, Allen simply saw it as sticking to the mission of loving God and doing as much good for people as he could. Once you know your mission, you never depart from it.

CHAPTER SEVENTEEN

BUILDING ON TRUST

"First seek the Kingdom of God and His righteousness, and all these things will be added to you."

—*Matthew 6:33*

As a transportation broker, Allen never owned his own trucks for shipping freight. His entire company was built on people trusting him to be able to do what he said he could do. In the early days, business was done with a verbal agreement and a handshake. Even as the transportation logistics industry grew, and business was conducted with formalized policies and written contracts, the fundamentals of trust between brokers and customers remained the same.

One day Allen received a call from Bob Rose, his manager in the San Francisco office. Bob joined Allen Lund Company in March of 1986 and became one of Allen's most trusted long-standing employees as well as a friend. Working with Allen for as long as he had, Bob attested to the notion that faith and trust were the fuel that powered Allen's entire company.

This particular call had nothing to do with business. Bob had taken his daughter up to the University of Portland to tour the college. While there, Bob stopped to admire the newly constructed bell tower which was now the focal point of the entire campus. Bob complimented Allen on his work and jested that since he had worked for Allen for so long, one or two of those bricks were invariably his. Bob and Allen always had a light rapport between them. They could tease each other personally and also be very straightforward and unvarnished while communicating professionally.

Although Bob was making a joke, Allen was quick to agree with him. Allen earnestly felt that everything he was able to accomplish was due to the incredible and hardworking people surrounding him. So Allen jovially complimented Bob on his contribution and the conversation continued on casually. However, the truth was that while Bob stood in the shade of that enormous bell tower he was surprised by his emotions. As a Jewish man, Bob belonged to a different faith tradition and never anticipated getting choked up standing on the grounds of a Catholic university looking at a tower holding up an enormous iron cross. However, that tower was the physical embodiment of Allen's exceptional generosity. It was powerful to know Allen personally and simultaneously see the magnitude of the impact he was making in the world.

Allen was a lot like the bell tower he helped build. He was tall, hard to miss, and dedicated to his faith. Allen was also as consistent and reliable as the bells that rang out from the heart of the tower. While Allen made no sermons, his peaceful presence was a reminder of what God can do in the life of a man willing to follow Him.

Although Bob and Allen had different religious affiliations, Bob admired Allen's commitment to faith and the personal integrity it imbued into his life. When people discuss integrity they tend to focus on the quality of being honest and morally upright. Allen certainly exemplified these qualities, but there is another more profound understanding of the word, which is the quality of being whole and undivided, integrated and structurally sound. This second definition provides a greater insight into the way Allen led his life.

Nothing about Allen was compartmentalized. How he did one thing was how he did everything. Who he was in one setting was the same as who he was everywhere else. He may have had many projects, many roles, and many goals, but everything fell under the same mission: First, seek the Kingdom of God and live righteously, and everything else will be added to you. This creed is a directive found in the Gospel of Saint Matthew and Allen believed in it. Allen may have articulated this Biblical principle in a more folksy way, like when telling his children, "Go to church, and everything else will work out alright." However, fundamentally, Allen wanted to put God at the front and center of everything he did, including the way he led his company.

In a literal way, Allen put his faith first at work. Meetings were opened with prayer. Mass was often offered at company board meetings and annual manager meetings. Allen also had a priest present for the duration of the gatherings. This was a subtle reminder to everyone on the Board to keep God in the midst of their conversations and decisions. Allen wanted to make sure this bold and visible display of faith didn't result in any legal issues for the company. He sought advice and counsel from Tim Busch, an attorney, businessman, and fellow member of Legatus. Tim assured Allen that as long as people knew that all prayers and religious activities were invitational and not mandatory, Allen Lund Company could continue to offer these opportunities. So Allen proceeded to openly display his faith, talk about it, and keep it as the guide of the company culture.

You certainly didn't have to be a Catholic to be a valued part of Allen Lund Company, you just had to display good character and treat people the right way. This was a standard Allen also held himself to.

Bob Rose recalls a time Allen called him to apologize for being short-tempered on a conference call the previous day.

Bob hadn't been dwelling on it; the incident was pretty mild. So Bob tried to assure Allen that an apology wasn't necessary. However, Allen insisted. He explained that at the time of their call, he had just learned that his grandson, Joseph, was going to have to undergo heart surgery. The news was weighing on him, but Allen explained that regardless of the circumstance, it wasn't an excuse for his tone and temper. The fact Allen took the time to call and apologize always stood out to Bob. It wasn't something most CEOs would have done, and it demonstrated Allen's integrity to hold himself to the standard his faith required of him.

Early mornings before work began, employees would sometimes walk into the office and find Allen finishing a private devotional reading containing scripture and prayers. The habit was evidence of Allen's humble pursuit of God's wisdom.

Allen sought God's guidance on how to be the kind of leader he felt called to be. This entailed being mindful of his words, actions, and attitudes toward others.

Allen not only believed that if you put God first, everything else in your business would fall into place, but he also believed if you hire good people with good ethics and family values, you could trust them to do a good job. Allen had no desire to micromanage any of the people he hired. He believed if you give good people the right tools and support, they will create the systems and practices that work for them and the company as a whole.

In 1998, Allen received a letter and resume in the mail from a man named Jim McGuire. Jim had previously been working for a competitor and was looking for a new start. Allen called Jim a few days later. After a couple of conversations, Allen flew to Charlotte, North Carolina, to meet Jim and discuss opening an office there. Allen and Jim sat down to dinner with a bottle of wine and talked for four hours. Only twenty-five minutes of the dinner were spent discussing business credentials; for the other three and a half hours, Allen asked questions about Jim's life, family, and upbringing. Unlike other job interviews, Jim felt completely relaxed; the conversation was easy and unforced as if he'd known Allen his whole life. Allen however was strategically finding out who Jim was at his core. If someone's heart was in the right place and they had a strong work ethic, Allen could trust them to do business the right way. At the end of the successful meeting, Jim asked Allen what his next step was. Allen told him to find an office space, and then they would send him some computers and phones. That was it. There would be very little red tape and a lot of autonomy going forward.

Allen built the structure of the company on this kind of freedom. He looked for trailblazers, self-starters, and encouraged them to forge their own paths. Allen built a profit-sharing model that allowed branch offices to keep a large percentage of their profits. Regardless of each office's success or struggles, the percentage never changed and remained constant throughout the years. In this way, Allen preserved and promoted the entrepreneurial spirit that he felt was instrumental to a successful company. He incentivized hard work by placing no caps or limits on what his people could make or accomplish.

Allen's leadership style was simple, and he passed it on to Jim and the other managers. First, he made sure the people working for him knew what he expected. He then gave them whatever support they needed to help them succeed. Finally, he got out of the way and let them figure out the specifics. He certainly kept an eye on things after that, celebrating employees who did well and holding people accountable when they could do better, but this simple approach built a thriving and motivated team.

Everyone respected Allen as a leader and felt empowered by the trust he placed in them. There was a consensus among the managers: no one ever wanted to let Allen down. He had become a father figure and mentor to so many people at the company. Tracey Lewin was one of the employees who particularly felt this way.

Tracey started at ALC on January 9, 1989. Her mother had worked in the same building as Allen in La Canada and leased office space from him before the entire building was converted to operate exclusively as ALC's headquarters. All Tracey's mother knew at the time was that her daughter needed a job, and Allen Lund was a good landlord and a very nice man. Tracey took her mother's advice and called Allen. That same day, Allen invited her to come into the office for an interview. Tracey's resume included a litany of odd jobs she'd been working since she was fifteen years old. She was nervous walking into the office because she didn't know anything about the business, or even what kind of job she was looking for. Allen glanced at her resume for a few moments, threw the paper over his shoulder, and said, "Tell me about you."

Allen hired Tracey on the spot. She was brave, transparent, and audacious, qualities Allen respected and so he found a starting position for her in the accounting department. The moment the resume was thrown over Allen's shoulder, Tracey realized she wasn't limited or defined by the words on the page. Allen became a mentor who believed in her and helped her believe in herself. While Tracey often went to Allen for advice, when issues at work came up, Allen's replies would sometimes frustrate her. He would constantly say things like, "I know you'll find a way" or "Well, sounds like you have a problem, go figure it out." After working for him for a few years, Tracey realized it was Allen's way of empowering her to be a problem-solver. Having faith in people means committing to letting them grow. They can't grow to their full potential without being trusted with the space to learn and accomplish small victories on their own.

Even with the forced lessons in independence, Tracey had an assurance of just how much Allen cared about her. His door was always open, and over the years, she came to that door when needing guidance, both professionally and personally. Allen trusted his team with abundant freedom, but he remained extremely invested in people's lives. Allen knew if people were doing well in their home lives, that would naturally affect everything else they did, including their work. This is partly why Allen always started conversations with his employees with questions like, "What's going on in your world?" Allen learned a lot about people by what kind of information they chose to tell him first. He'd proceed to ask about their family, starting with the topics closest to their hearts and then work his way outward to business topics. This was how Allen took people's metaphorical temperature. Everyone working for Allen knew he cared about them— their aspirations and their futures.

Allen and Kathie had already committed to providing the best healthcare for their employees and all of their dependents, but over the years, they also started 401K matching. They began with a nickel to every dollar and increased the amount incrementally until Allen Lund Company contributed a $0.40 match to every dollar an employee placed in their retirement fund. The Lunds also started an employee stock purchase plan so employees had the opportunity to own a piece of what they were working so hard for. The value of these stocks dramatically appreciated over time, and buying in has become a highly sought-after opportunity. Employees ready to retire sell back their stocks to the company for an additional retirement bonus.

Allen and Kathie were most proud of the employee benefits they were able to offer. They put people over profits because it was the right thing to do, but the byproduct of this meant good employees wanted to stay, and ALC kept its incredible talent. The goal was for ALC to be the type of company employees could spend their entire careers if they wanted. Allen believed the best way to make a difference in someone's life was to provide them with an opportunity to work and create a good future for themselves and their loved ones. Allen's goal was to help people advance as far as they wanted to go.

Allen never minded people who asked for more opportunities to grow within the company. In these meetings, Allen asked a lot of questions and challenged people, but he appreciated the initiative and often rewarded it. Tracey Lewin came to Allen one day for a conversation about moving up to take on a bigger role at ALC. After hearing her out, Allen asked, "Okay, but who will take your place?"

It was a common question he asked in conversations like these. If people wanted to grow, they needed to be training the team under them to be ready to fill their shoes. It wasn't long before Allen started to think about that question for himself. As he got older and the company grew larger, Allen was more aware year by year of just how many people were depending on him and the company as a whole. It was imperative he take steps to ensure the company could run just as well without him.

Allen had no plan to retire, but he still understood he couldn't be around forever.

Allen took the first step to ensure the longevity of the company when he promoted his sons to vice presidents and brought Eddie back to California. Allen had expanded their roles and they were already running most of the day-to-day operations, but the proximity to all of his sons in one office gave him the privilege of mentoring them into the leaders who would carry the company forward into the future. The mentorship developed organically. Every morning David, Kenny, Eddie, and Allen's son-in-law, Steve, now the CFO, would meet with Allen, drink coffee, and talk about the company. It wasn't an official meeting with a scheduled time. They would all just float in and out of Allen's office and brief him on what was on their dockets for the day. The casual habit became an important time where together, they worked through problems, asked important questions, and voiced their opinions.

Eventually, Allen formalized this habit and created an Executive Committee to serve as the guiding decision-making body for the company. He appointed his sons, Steve Doerfler, and Chetan Tandon, the CIO, to sit on this committee. Talking through issues pertaining to the company afforded all of the members the opportunity to hear Allen's thoughts and learn from his approach to solving a myriad of issues. However, Allen didn't dominate the group. He wanted everyone to feel they had a voice and insisted that all major decisions were made by consensus. If they couldn't agree, they would keep discussing until they were united on the topic.

One of the many topics discussed was the future direction the company would take as it grew. The group decided to slate a handful of talented employees they felt would soon be ready to be promoted to vice presidents. Jim McGuire, Bob Rose, and Tracey Lewin were all discussed, as well as Lenny Sciarappa, who was at that time managing the Boston office. Every one of these individuals had distinguished themselves over the years as natural leaders who would add diverse opinions and new innovative ways of doing things at the top level.

Still, the question remained on who would take Allen's place one day. This wasn't something Allen wanted to solely decide on. In addition to the executive committee, Allen had also added to the members of the Board of Directors. The original Board included Allen, Kathie, their six children, Terry Walker, the Director of HR, Steve Asip, the long term manager of the Atlanta Office, Dennis Connors the original manager of the San Francisco office, and Joe Hillman the company's first CFO. Allen slowly added members to the Board and filled seats when other members retired. In 2004 Bill Bess, manager of the Orlando office, joined the ranks. When Joe Hillman retired in 2006, and Steve Doerfler was promoted to CFO, he also filled the seat on the Board. Eventually, Allen asked Bob Rose, Chetan Tandon, and Jim McGuire to serve as well.

When Allen called Jim McGuire in 2014 and asked if he would also consider joining the board, Jim initially hesitated, which Allen noticed on the phone. When pressed, Jim explained he was hesitant because he wasn't a "yes-man" who could simply agree and go along with the group. Allen said that was the precise reason he had asked him to join. Allen wanted people who he could trust to tell him the truth about what was going on in the company. Jim's ability to see things differently was a strength and Allen felt that would add a lot of value to the Board. It was important to Allen to get the right people on the Board of Directors because, ultimately, these were the individuals he trusted to one day select Allen Lund Company's next leader.

Perhaps the greatest act of faith any leader can make is surrendering control over the thing that they've built to ensure it can continue to thrive beyond them. Once Allen had great leaders in place and others slated to soon join their ranks, he realized he needed to personally ensure his family and his company were protected financially. He contacted Tim Busch again, who had experience helping large companies prepare to pass on to the next generation. Under Tim's guidance, Allen and Kathie transferred ownership of the company to a family trust so it would not be in his estate when they passed away. He also placed his estate and remaining voting shares in the company into a trust and made his family members the beneficiaries. Tim explained that many companies are forced to sell in order to pay steep estate taxes, and so surrendering ownership would protect the company's long-term well-being and safeguard his family's ownership.

Few leaders are willing to relinquish control of something they've worked so hard to create. However, Allen trusted his family and the people he mentored. He would still be leading the charge for as long as God enabled him to, operating as CEO, but Allen Lund Company didn't belong to him anymore. This wasn't something that bothered him. He knew it was the right thing to do for the company, and doing the right thing was how he always did business. He started ALC to feed his family, and now, thanks to Tim Busch's help with the restructuring, the company would continue to feed his family and all the families who worked with them, for years to come.

Just like Allen truly did feel like Bob Rose made some of the bricks in the Belltower possible, Allen felt that the company had been built by hundreds of incredible hardworking people. He may have started it, but it had now grown into something bigger than him. This was all because he worked hard, put good-hearted people in place, and gave them the tools, incentives, and freedom they needed to build something spectacular. The company was a part of them now, too. Allen's wisdom, humility, and, most importantly, his faith ensured Allen Lund Company was now ready to outlast him.

CHAPTER EIGHTEEN

GRADING A SLICE OF HEAVEN

"As I stood on the rim of this canyon one snowy night, the vision I had, Oh, what a sight!"

—Dennis Guyman,
Excerpt from the the poem "Stake My Claim"

It seemed Allen was never without a building project. From the earliest days of his time at St. Francis High School, he consistently answered the call to help various Catholic missions revitalize their infrastructure. When he saw a need, he volunteered his talents. There was one call, however, that came from his own inner voice expressing a desire he had for a long time.

Allen always dreamed of owning a piece of Utah. Growing up there, he felt a special connection to the land. He enjoyed going back to Utah to visit his family and old friends. Deer hunting season was another good excuse to depart from the hustle and bustle of Los Angeles and hike through the Utah wilderness with loved ones. Allen particularly enjoyed hunting with Harold Felgar, his grizzly cigar-chomping neighbor at the old ALC office in downtown LA. Harold hunted with a group of friends in San Juan County, near the Four Corners where the Utah, Colorado, Arizona, and New Mexico borders come together. This is a place where it's possible to stand in all four states at the same time. Allen fell in love with the rugged terrain, chasms, cliffs, and canyons of this high desert paradise. In 2001, he began to scout land for sale in the area.

The weather in San Juan County is varied. One winter day Allen and Kathie hopped on the back of a snowmobile to survey Long Canyon Ranch, a remote 300-acre plot of land between the Utah towns of Blanding and Monticello. The couple marveled at its beauty. The canyon had a clear view of the Abajo Mountain and the property backed up to cliffs where the ancient Anasazi Native American Tribe, who lived on the land in 1300 AD, had carved dwellings into the cliffside. Nestled in the middle of this majestic scenery was a tiny old homesteader cabin, which Allen felt was a perfect camp for future hunting expeditions. The Lunds agreed this was the place they wished to stake their claim.

Allen purchased Long Canyon Ranch and started a yearly hunting tradition with his sons and close friends. Each October for mule deer season, they would use the one-bedroom cabin as a base camp. When they first bought the ranch, the cabin was uninhabitable. So they spent the first summer cleaning it out so it could be safely used. The cabin still had no running water, kitchen, or bathroom. If they needed to go, there was an outhouse within eye-shot. Showers were initially non-existent at the ranch, so Allen usually rented a hotel in town for everyone to get cleaned up. In the early years of this hunting tradition, Allen's sons pitched tents and camped at the ranch. "Roughing it" was part of their fun. However, Allen and his friends still drove back to the hotel each night. He loved the great outdoors, but he also liked sleeping in a comfortable bed. The group of men bonded around this annual tradition. They returned to Los Angeles with Utah dirt on their boots and big smiles on their faces.

However, Allen dreamed of carving out this piece of land to build a place where the whole family could come and have a comfortable sanctuary away from Los Angeles. Allen's friend, Hayden Eaves, owned a large lodge-style home in Montana with rustic and rugged architecture that paralleled its surrounding landscape. In his mind's eye, Allen could imagine a similar home built at Long Canyon, spacious with a homespun feeling. The dream was a long-term goal, but he set plans in motion. As a heavy equipment operator, Allen knew this dream would require a lot of work atop a bulldozer to carve out and level the land for building. Before anything else, he wanted to fix up their tiny cabin. He purchased a steel Quonset shed kit and put it together with David, Kenny, and Eddie. It would store equipment and tools for the upcoming project. It served its purpose but Allen almost immediately needed more space for larger equipment.

He hired a building contractor to help with the updates to the cabin and draw up plans for a larger green garage. They argued with Allen, who insisted on doing his own grading for the building project. This wasn't what the contractor preferred. He believed this would delay their progress and his team would have to redo the work. As the client and landowner, Allen got to do what he wanted. He was happiest when aboard a piece of equipment. Working outdoors with his hands was an opportunity he never wanted to miss.

Most graders require a transit level and ground stakes to show them where the land is uneven. Allen was old school, so he graded the land with his bulldozer and did everything by eye. Allen's finished grade was perfect and the contractor marveled at the work. He brought Allen a check, refunding part of the money Allen had already paid. The contractor had assumed his team would need to redo Allen's work and therefore factored in extra time and labor in his original invoice. When he realized the land was perfectly level and ready for building, he returned the money. The builders put in a large green garage behind the Quonset shed and also ran a gas line and running water to the cabin.

Long Canyon Ranch is sandwiched by and equidistant to the neighboring small towns of Blanding and Monticello, whose combined population does not exceed five thousand. Like many towns of this size, most people know each other and news travels fast. So the residents didn't quite know what to make of the California businessman coming to buy up Utah land. Pretty quickly, however, any preconceived notions people had about Allen Lund would shift. Allen loved to ride into town and have breakfast each morning. This was how he started to make friends in Blanding. He would strike up conversations with locals and find out what line of business they were in. Allen was determined to engage as many local businesses as possible to source materials and craftsmen for the building projects at the ranch. He began to earn a reputation for being friendly and for paying his accounts on time. Allen's firm commitment to hiring within the community would also stimulate the local economy.

One day Allen went into Blanding to talk to Steve Francom, who owned a flooring and window treatment business. Allen wanted blinds for the homesteader cabin. He walked into Steve's shop on Main Street in work boots and dirty blue jeans, not at all the picture of the "Californian" Steve was expecting. It turned out Steve Francom did more than just blinds. His name was already on a list Allen's friend, Kelly Laws, had made of potential builders in the area Allen should consider hiring. When he realized the connection, Allen showed Steve a picture of his friend's home in Montana and invited Steve to come see the ranch. Steve drew up a proposal, and his vision for the house won Allen over. He hired Steve to build his dream home.

The first day, Allen told Steve to hop on his bulldozer and go with him to do some work. Allen rode as a passenger and asked Steve to drive. Steve was shocked to so quickly be trusted to drive this large and expensive piece of equipment, but Allen acted like it was no big deal. He teased Steve about not realizing the engine needed to warm up before turning the ignition. Steve was quiet and reserved by nature, but realized quickly Allen only teased the people he liked. Steve felt this was the day he was adopted by Allen Lund, who would from this moment forward treat Steve like one of his own sons.

If Steve had any trepidation about working for the successful California businessman whose name he heard around town, it all melted away when he watched Allen work. Allen would fly in, take off his suit and tie, throw on his blue jeans, and by the end of the day he'd be covered in more dirt and grease than any other worker there. No one could keep up with Allen, much less outwork him. When grading the land for the ranch house, Steve would run the loader and Allen ran his bulldozer. Allen would have four more mounds of dirt waiting for Steve when he finished carrying off one load. Steve worked as quickly as he could to keep up, but it was impossible. Allen would flash him a cheeky smile as if to say, "What's taking you so long?"

The house was a beautiful two story western style ranch

made with stone and other natural materials. There was a covered porch, outdoor fireplace, and large windows that let in ample light and allowed the Lunds to admire the outdoor spendors. Inside the home everything was as big as Allen was. The ceilings, doorways, and furniture were all tall, fitting for the man who earned the nickname "Big Al." The design included a large kitchen with a long farmer's table, big enough for the whole family. A floor-to-ceiling stone fireplace became the center of the home and the living room had plenty of seating for a rapidly growing family. It was exquisite and the Lunds were very pleased with the finished product. To celebrate the finish, Allen and Kathie hosted a large party for everyone in town who worked on the home. They all brought their families to tour the completed project, and together they enjoyed a cookout with live music and dancing.

Steve Francom's business would never be the same, and Allen would hire him for every addition he added to the property. Additionally, all of the cabinets, furniture, flooring, and labor were sourced locally. Allen's dream was beneficial to many small businesses.

Allen was very aware of the impact he could have on the community, both directly and indirectly, and he was committed to do as much good as he could with the resources God had given him. In Allen's trademark under-the-radar way, he engaged in many quiet acts of kindness for the people in town. Steve

Francom worked with a man named Dennis, who had a lot of issues with his teeth. The issues were deeper than just cosmetic and profoundly affected his quality of life. Allen paid for his dental work and it changed his entire personality. Previously, Dennis never smiled and barely talked to anyone. When he got his new teeth he smiled, chatted, and engaged with people with a new sense of confidence and joy.

Steve Francom always felt he could call Allen when he learned of someone in need. Steve was Mormon and some of the members of his church were looking for a service project to do. There was a widow in town with three children. One of her children was handicapped and the house they lived in had fallen into disrepair. It needed to be gutted and redone, but the woman didn't have the financial resources to do this on her own. Steve had the knowledge to pull off the project and the young men in his group were willing to donate their time for labor, but they still needed the materials. Steve called Allen, who asked for a plan to be drawn up, along with a list of needs. This was the usual drill with Allen. He was eager to do good, but he asked all of the questions first. Allen knew how important a clear vision and cohesive plan was to any project, and he wouldn't contribute anything until those elements were in place.

Allen responded to Steve's plan with the dollar amount he would provide. It wasn't the number Steve was originally hoping for, but Steve was grateful to Allen for contributing all the same. They fixed the woman's house, which changed her life and made her proud to invite friends to her home; something she hadn't done in a long time. It turned out that the amount Allen gave was what was required to get it done - not a dime over or under. Steve marveled at Allen's accuracy, but at this point Allen had overseen so many renovation projects he was skilled at knowing how far a dollar would go.

Allen's barometer for measuring when and what to give came down to the question of whether the contribution would strengthen its recipient. Allen wanted to imbue people with strength and help them restore and maintain their dignity. In the aforementioned examples, Allen stepped in with uncommon generosity for people who couldn't otherwise afford what they desperately needed.

However, help from Allen could come in many ways. After Steve finished Allen's house, Steve started on another large contract. Unfortunately not all clients were as honest as Allen. After 80 percent of the work was finished, the client stopped paying. Steve was forced to walk away from the contract altogether; the first and only time he had to do so in his career. He took an enormous financial hit and was scared he and his family would lose everything. Allen and Steve talked on the phone every day. Even after the Long Canyon house was finished, Allen called Steve to check in on him. When Steve told Allen about the situation, Allen had many questions for him. Desperate and afraid, Steve hoped Allen might offer to step in and help him financially, but Allen never did. He instead offered to fly over the building project in the company plane and see what a bag of flour would do to it if dropped from one thousand feet.

All jesting aside, Allen called Steve and encouraged him through the entire ordeal. Whenever he felt Steve was disheartened he would say, "Don't get your gander down." Allen was known for his use of a lot of old country phrases like this, but no one knew the origins of these one-liners. In this case, he was just trying to tell Steve not to lose his courage. The ups and downs of life help carve us into the people God calls us to be. From Allen's point of view, all challenges were just opportunities to grow. Steve eventually pulled through and business bounced back. He felt Allen modeled God's love to him through the whole situation. God, a good Father, doesn't bail us out of every hardship, but He does give us the strength to get through them and promises to walk with us in all of life's peaks and valleys. Steve felt he learned a lot from this difficult season, and the lessons he learned helped him navigate future challenges. Yet it was Allen's encouragement that buttressed him through it all.

Both personally and professionally Allen had walked through his own peaks and valleys. Set backs, recessions, and hardships didn't frighten him. He had been in business long enough to realize the ebbs and flows of the market. When the 2008 recession hit, Allen once again looked for the opportunities hidden in the chaos. Optimistic and undaunted, he started several new building projects on the ranch. He wanted a guest house, attached garage for cars, and a large barn for his biggest pieces of equipment. The projects kept people's businesses afloat and put food on their tables in a difficult season.

Allen, his sons, and his hunting buddies enjoyed the ranch in the early years of Allen owning it. They navigated the land by their past shared experiences. They'd say things like, "I'm going to go hunt out where Joe shot that deer" or "I'll be near Eddie's rock." There were two ways to get a landmark named after you. You either had to pull off an impressive shot in a location or simply go there often enough to have the group associate the place with you. Eddie's rock, for example, was a place he would often disappear to. It was an easy place for him to find before dawn and it gave him a good vantage point of the meadow. The group's map was their rote history of good times spent together. The reason Allen wanted to expand the house, add a guesthouse, and build additional rooms on the perimeter of the barn was so his entire family could gather and participate in the fun. He wanted his six children, their spouses, and his twenty-two grandchildren to have a place to stay. Allen and Kathie added bunk beds in some of the rooms so they could accommodate everyone.

The ranch became the epicenter of fun. There were games, sports, adventures riding four wheelers, and big family meals. They took turns with things like cooking, doing dishes, and cleaning. The family even found ways to make those chores fun. They'd blast music and sing along while forming an assembly line washing and drying dishes. The grandchildren loved being able to play with all of their cousins, and especially enjoyed time with their grandfather. Allen found creative ways to entertain them. On the dirt roads leading back to the ranch all of the grandchildren would pile into Allen's truck. There was a button on the dash that read "Power Slide." In reality the button simply slid open the window between the cab and bed of the pick-up. However, the kids thought it caused the entire truck to skid along the path. The grandkids would excitedly chant, "power slide, power slide!" from the backseat, and Allen would hit the button and the brakes simultaneously. The truck would slide along the dirt road causing a huge cloud of dust to be kicked up around them. Like a true showman, he sold the performance well, turning the wheel into each hydroplane and creating a make-shift rollercoaster for the giggling children.

Every grandchild had stories like this and can remember their grandfather giving them a ride on his equipment. Allen was like a kid himself while on the ranch. He drove up and down paths where no one else would dare go. He loved to prank the kids as well. When he put a pond on his property, he purchased an amphibious vehicle. Allen took several grandchildren out on his new ride, but he didn't tell them it was viable on both land and water. He pretended to slide down the hill towards the pond, saying they were going too fast to stop. The grandchildren felt certain they'd crash and sink into the pond. A mixture of shock and relief washed over them as the vehicle cruised on the surface of the water. Allen couldn't contain his laughter.

Allen kept his largest equipment in the new barn Steve Francom built. Like the other buildings on the ranch, the design reflected Allen's dream for the place. The barn had doors like an airplane hanger and a sand floor that made it easy for Allen to maneuver his equipment in and out of the space. When the grandkids were at the ranch, they liked to play volleyball inside the barn on the sand floor. Allen shifted all of his machines over to one side of the barn to give them space to set up their net and court. It was a small gesture, but in the end, the action was a powerful metaphor for how Allen made space in his dream for other people. Allen's biggest joy in life was watching his family have fun and enjoy each other. For this reason Allen was rarely the center of attention at family gatherings. He had a chair in the corner of the room where he could sit back and watch the beautiful chaos.

Christmas was the exception to this norm. Allen and Kathie invited everyone to the ranch every other year for the holiday and the tradition became known as "Ranch-mas." Allen loved

Christmas and always wanted to dole out the presents from under the tree. Unlike most people, he never just handed them out. He hurled them across the room to the recipients. Everyone needed to "think fast" to catch their gifts. Holidays were filled with lots of fun like this. The living room at the main house was chalked full of boardgames, books, checker sets, and musical instruments. In this sense, the house was one of the most sophisticated homes ever designed because it perfectly served its purpose without a hint of pretension. It had a homespun and down-to-earth quality, but every detail of the layout was meticulously designed to optimize comfort, community, and joy. Allen didn't usually join in on the games, preferring as always to sit back and watch the smiling faces of his family huddled together in the warmth of great love and the flames of the roaring fireplace.

CHAPTER NINETEEN

THREE YARDS AND A CLOUD OF DUST

"This project is about all of us and our time, talents, and treasures, and most of all prayers."

—*Allen Lund*

The ranch Allen and Kathie built was an extension of who they were. The couple possessed a work-hard-play-hard mentality when it came to family and marriage, so life at the ranch naturally reflected this balance. As more land became available, gradually Allen expanded his property to 1,275 acres. With the land, home, and building projects, there was always work to be done. Every time the family visited they'd embark on some productive joint undertaking, whether it was putting in fence posts or maintaining roads. Fun and enterprise became the brick-and-mortar that made Long Canyon Ranch the unique place it is today.

Faith was at the core of the Lund family, so even when they stepped away from their daily routines in Los Angeles and made the drive to their remote Utah getaway, they carried their convictions with them. Church attendance was paramount. They would load up their vehicles every Sunday and drive to St. Joseph Catholic Church, a small nearby parish in Monticello, Utah. It was a modest church with a little sanctuary. When the Lunds came to town and loaded into the church pews, it was like an alien invasion. The family was large in both number and physical stature. They also carried a palpable energy with them, unlike anything some of the parishioners had ever experienced.

The Lund family slowly became part of this small Utah community. Allen was active across a host of service projects in the area. Even the deer meat from his hunting expeditions went to local families who needed it. Anytime anyone presented an idea to Allen or asked him for his support, that person had to put together a strong plan of action before Allen would hop on board. He needed to understand their vision and make sure they had counted the cost of what it would take. He was a busy man, and he couldn't say "yes" to every idea someone presented, but he would always hear them out as they made their pitch.

The one person who always had Allen's ear was Kathie. Kathie had Allen's respect as well as his heart. They were married for fifty-eight years, and in their marriage they both did their best to make each other happy. Kathie brims with creativity and rivaled the voraciousness of Allen's industrious nature. The impetus of so much of what the family did and what happened on the ranch was Kathie's large heart and sense of fun. The couple complemented each other well. So much of what Allen was able to achieve was due to Kathie building a stable and loving home. Kathie trusted Allen without reservation, because she knew every decision he made was rooted in the commitment to honor God and cherish her. Although the two seldom disagreed, when they did Kathie deferred to her husband's wisdom. If he said "no" to something, she figured he had a good reason, but Allen rarely said no to Kathie Lund especially when he saw she was passionate about a project.

As they spent more time at the ranch, Allen's daughter Natalie realized St. Joseph didn't have a lot of programs for their young parishioners. She and her brother-in-law, Mike, discussed wanting to do something to help the parish while the family was in town for the summer. They brought the topic up to the entire family, who collectively felt called to give back to the community. Natalie, Anna, Christina, and Kenny all had experience working with young people. Natalie had been a teacher, Kenny and Christina had worked at camps, and Anna had previously led a bible camp at her church in California. In 2006, the family decided to start a Vacation Bible School, where young children could learn about Jesus in a summer camp environment. Kathie became the biggest champion of this idea. She asked Allen to talk to the priest about letting them run the program, which Allen did. Once they got approval Kathie ordered the materials and the entire family became involved in setting up games, making snacks, putting on skits, and teaching Bible lessons to children in the community. They hosted these camps at St. Joseph Church. Allen facilitated his family's dream of doing this, leaning into his preternatural talent: logistics.

During the camps, Allen always brought out a priest he was friends with to celebrate mass and be present to encourage the children. Allen was doing what he did best, managing logistics. He often invited members of the clergy to help with the camps, or simply to come to the ranch for a spiritual retreat. One year, Allen called his friend Mother Regina Marie, a Carmelite nun who was the Superior General of her order. He asked if she could send a couple of Sisters to the ranch to help teach the children. Mother Regina Marie agreed on one condition. The Carmelite Sisters attend mass daily as part of their lifestyle. She told Allen they would come and help with the Bible school, so long as Allen could ensure they were able to attend Mass each day they were there. He told her it wouldn't be a problem because St. Joseph Church was nearby and a priest celebrated Mass as part of their Vacation Bible School. So the Sisters hopped on a plane to come help. One morning, however, Allen got a call saying something had come up and there would be no Mass the following day. To keep his promise, Allen drove the sisters 300-mile-round trip to another church that was hosting Mass. The Sisters told him he didn't need to do that. They could simply spend some time in prayer as an alternative under the circumstances. However, Allen insisted. He had to keep his word.

Allen's integrity was his greatest Christian witness. He did not speak about his faith to very many people, but it deeply informed his way of life. He had a spiritual gift of administration and loved to create opportunities for other people to use their talents to serve God. All his building projects—whether it was the ranch, a school, or another Catholic mission—were his way of carving out places for people to encounter a little piece of Heaven. Kathie loved talking about God and the Bible. She enjoyed providing evangelistic opportunities. This is why she was so passionate about their Vacation Bible School continuing to thrive. The community also loved the camp. Parents not only saw how much their children were learning, but they also watched their kids come out of their shells and join in the skits with their peers. After Allen helped set up the camp, he would sit and enjoy watching his family use their gifts to pour into the community. St. Joseph Catholic Church was in poor condition. It was built in 1935 by sheepherding immigrants who wanted a place to worship. The foundation was crumbling and the log cabin that sat on the property behind the sanctuary had sunk into the earth and ruptured the building's gas line.

One day Allen sat at the back of a Vacation Bible School talent show with his friend Tom Corrao, a Deacon of the Catholic Church who served at St. Joseph. Allen told Tom that he intended to build the parish a new church. Not long after this conversation, Allen and Tom drove to Salt Lake City to speak to the Catholic Bishop and the Vicar General about building the new church. Tom marveled at the confident way Allen walked into their office and told them what he was going to do. He presented them with the plan and the way he wanted to fund it. Allen would donate to the archdiocese in Utah, but they agreed to set up a special fund so the money would be solely allocated to building St. Joseph. After this meeting, Tom asked Allen why he was doing this.

Allen replied, "Because I can, and because you need it."

St. Joseph needed more space, so they bought the lot behind the original church. The church didn't have much money to put towards the land, which would cost $57,000. Allen told Tom that if the church could manage the $7,000, he would help with the rest. It was important for everyone to be co-laborers in this endeavor. The church agreed and stretched to reach the goal. The entire project seemed like an enormous undertaking to Tom. He often asked Allen how he thought they could pull it off. Allen would tell him they'd get it done with "three yards and a cloud of dust." The expression came from football teams who rely on a running game. If a team gets three yards each play, they can get a first down. It's a moderate but consistent strategy. Allen believed the same philosophy applied to life.

You accomplish things little by little, so it's important to keep powering through every day.

In 2014, they broke ground for the new church. The project was funded largely by the Lunds. Steve Francom was brought on to design and build the project, and construction was completed in 2016. Now St. Joseph Catholic Church has an exquisite stone building with a gathering area, kitchen, and sanctuary that seats up to 150 people. The structure, with its stonework, large windows, steeple, and traditional design, is considered one of the most beautiful buildings in Monticello. A touching feature of the new church is the extra distance from the front pew and the steps of the altar. It was included so the children of the parish could have space to perform their Vacation Bible School skits inside the church.

Steve Francom did a lot of research in order to ensure the new St. Joseph's met all of the many specifications of the Catholic church. Fortunately he had gotten a chance to practice on a similar design he built for Allen at the ranch. Together Steve and Allen also built a small private chapel for the Lund family to gather together to pray. The chapel sat at the highest point of the property overlooking the house, a constant reminder to put God above all else. It had everything necessary to host Mass, and a ladder to a loft that had additional seating for grandchildren. The Lunds began using this sacred space for prayer, baptisms, and their yearly Christmas pageant tradition. Each Ranch-mas, the family walked up the stone steps leading from the house to the chapel and reenacted the nativity scene. The first couple of years were a ragamuffin manger scene complete with makeshift costumes. For the baby Jesus, they took a butternut squash from the greenhouse and wrapped it in swaddling clothes. As the years went by and new grandbabies were born, they would take over the role, drastically improving the production's realism.

Prayer was at the center of all Lund Family gatherings, so Allen and Kathie spent time beautifying the inside of the chapel. They commissioned four stained glass windows, three in the front of the chapel and one at the back. The largest window was of Christ the Redeemer, flanked by Mary and St. Joseph on each side. All of the stained glass features tiny tributes to Utah. The flowers at Mary's feet are native to the land, and the portrait of Joseph shows him working at a carpenter's table inside his home. Out of the window inside the picture, you can see Monument Valley. The border of each stained glass also features various designs found inside the cliff dwellings of the ancient Puebleans who once inhabited the land.

The stained glass image at the back of the church features the image of St. Kateri Tekakwitha, the first Native American to be canonized as a saint in the Catholic Church. The selection of this saint was indicative of the impact Allen had on the surrounding community. Allen had a unifying effect in San Juan County, which suffers from substantial division along racial and religious lines. Allen didn't see divisions, he just saw people. This freed him to build bridges between various groups. For example, Allen's friend Steve Francom, who was like a son to him, was a Morman who built a Catholic church. That was a radical bit of news for some people in the community, but for Allen, it was as normal as picking the best man for the job.

In some ways, Allen was very intentional about healing divides. Looking to help even in small ways. San Juan County includes part of the Navajo Nation. The Native Americans who live on the reservation often feel unseen by their neighbors. Generational hurt for both communities runs deep. A lot of the deer meat Allen had processed he sent to families on the reservation. Allen also had an appreciation for the art and history of the Native population in the area. With the help of a local curator, Allen purchased art from Navajo artisans who preserved ancestral techniques like basket weaving. Then Allen adorned his Utah home with these items. Allen would walk into the Blue Mountain Trading Post in town and ask a lot of questions about where each piece of art was from and which local artist made each item. Allen liked the idea of supporting these artists just like he supported many local businesses in town. He used his resources to encourage new things to grow.

Today the ranch is like a museum of local talent. This is just another way the ranch became the outward embodiment of Allen's inner nature to love his neighbors. Long Canyon

Ranch was the opus Allen never realized he composed. It became a special place for the Lund family, so dear that several of Allen's granddaughters decided to get married there. Retreats were also hosted at the ranch for various groups the family supported. Allen and Kathie used the ranch to bring people together, creating space for them to learn about one another, enjoy themselves, and to spend time in the beauty of God's creation. Most of all the ranch was a place where everyone felt welcome, where friends became family, and where Allen gave people opportunities to use their God-given talents. Sometimes that talent was a grandchild playing guitar and singing in the chair next to him. Sometimes the talent was a young builder designing his masterpiece. Sometimes the talent was Kathie and the Lund children embracing their community by teaching them about the love of God. Through all of it, Allen's utmost joy was uplifting the people around him and watching them flourish.

Allen's greatest sermon was in the way he led his life. In grand gestures and in small moments, he would consistently bring everything back to the simple aim of loving God and others well. It is how he accomplished so much. It's why his marriage and family became an effervescent font, flowing with life-giving joy and energy. He showed up each day with that simple commitment and built this little slice of heaven on earth with three yards and a cloud of dust.

CHAPTER TWENTY
PEACHES

"No man knows the hour of his ending, nor can he choose the place or manner of his going. To each it is given to die proudly, to die well, and this is, indeed, the final measure of the man."

—*Louis L'Amour*

Even as he aged, Allen didn't slow down. He was once asked why he didn't permanently move to the ranch and enjoy a quiet retired life. Allen responded that living full time at the ranch was impossible because it would mean missing too many events. He was referring to the activities of his twenty-two grandchildren. Cheering them on from the stands was one of his favorite pastimes. But Allen was also in constant vocational demand with the company and various boards he chaired. Besides, retirement was simply not on his radar. Even when he was at the ranch, he was still on a company conference call at least once a day.

By this time, Allen had restructured the company and the next generation of Lunds were taking on greater responsibilities.

However, Allen's involvement in the company did not wane. He still went into the office every day, keeping his hand on the pulse of the company. He wanted to see ALC continue to thrive and make an even greater impact on the industry as well as the community. When Allen Lund Company celebrated its fortieth year in business, Allen challenged each sales and support office to do an act of kindness in their communities. The first year the company as a whole completed seventy-six service projects across the country. The tradition continues each year with every ALC branch office working with their own teams to serve the specific needs of their communities. There was nothing more exhilarating to Allen than coming together with other like-minded colleagues to do something good in the world. He was never more proud of his company. If anything, these acts of kindness inspired Allen to continue to speed up, not slow down.

Although stepping away from work into retirement did not appeal to Allen, as he got older he found more time to travel with Kathie. They went around Europe, hopped on several cruises, took in breathtaking landscapes in Alaska, visited the Vatican, and embarked on a study tour of Israel where the couple walked the same steps Christ walked on the earth. The first century archeological sites left a huge impression on Allen and Kathie. Their trip to the Holy Land would deepen their faith and forever illuminate their understanding of scripture.

Many of these trips were arranged by the various Catholic

organizations to which they belonged. Kathie and Allen had found an amazing group of friends through their involvement in these organizations; friendships that were solidified through their shared love for building the Kingdom of God. For example, Legatus is a non-profit membership organization designed for Catholic business leaders who are committed to engage and spread their faith. Allen and Kathie attended Legatus dinners once a month, which included Mass, fellowship, and the presence of a dynamic Catholic speaker. Allen had become friends with Tom Monaghan (the organization's founder), Father Robert Spitzer (the presiding National Chaplain), and many other chapter members including Tim Busch and Bill Close.

The Lunds linked arms with these friends to do some extraordinary things for the Catholic faith. Along with other Legatus members, Allen served on the committee responsible for the construction of the new Los Angeles Cathedral: the Cathedral of Our Lady of the Angels. With a capacity of three thousand, the new downtown structure featured contemporary design elements with massive bronze doors and tall alabaster windows that let ample natural light into a sanctuary. Allen specifically oversaw the construction of the Cathedral's parking structure, which he was happy to do because people had a lot less staunch opinions about parking garages than they did about sanctuaries. Construction for the LA Cathedral, a $189.7 million project, began in 1998 and was completed in 2002.

That same year Bill Close and several other chapter members of Legatus attended the National Prayer Breakfast in Washington D.C. and were inspired to do something similar in Los Angeles. The following year Allen and Kathie also made a trip to Washington to attend the breakfast with their friends Tom and Margie Romano. They agreed that Los Angeles needed a similar event, and now that the Cathedral was built, it should be filled with as much prayer as possible.

The idea to start a prayer breakfast marinated for a while. The Lunds and Romanos talked at length about how the event should be structured and eventually Allen reached out to Cardinal Mahony to obtain his endorsement. On September 19, 2006 the first annual Los Angeles Prayer Breakfast was hosted at the cathedral. It was a roaring success, with over eight hundred people in attendance. Allen invited Father Spitzer who was still the presiding chaplain of Legatus and President of Gonzaga University to give the keynote address. The Cathedral was filled with the prayers of people interceding for their city and their country. It started early in the morning so attendees could make it to work on time after the closing remarks. At Allen's request, the event closed with the collective singing of "God Bless America." The Prayer Breakfast continues to this day with annual attendance approaching two thousand. Allen chaired this event for twelve years, and the Romanos continue to chair the Prayer Breakfast to this day.

There is a famous story in the Old Testament that recounts the escapades of King David and his mighty men, who together accomplished extraordinary feats for the kingdom. Allen and his friends were a similar force in the modern world, doing more together than they could on their own. They were friends who didn't just enjoy each other; they were on a shared mission. However, Allen would have never considered himself a leader among them. It didn't matter how many boards he chaired, how large the company grew, or how many honors he was presented, Allen would simply say "I used to be a truck driver and now I'm just an old truck driver." Allen's goal was to come alongside this talented group of business leaders, often supporting their visions, to do as much good as possible with his time on Earth. As the years went by, Allen's commitment to do more and more for God only grew.

Allen's friend, Tim Busch felt called to reach people beyond Legatus, which focused primarily on inspiring business leaders. He didn't exactly know what that would look like, but he was eager to collaborate with Father Spitzer whose wealth of spiritual depth and theological knowledge was an edifying force for the faith.

The first response to this call was to organize spiritual retreats for individuals who desired to grow closer to God in a focused time of prayer. He hosted his first retreat at the DoubleTree Hotel in Irvine, California and Allen was in attendance. Eucharistic

Adoration was built into the retreat and each participant was assigned an hour of time for intentional prayer, collectively sustaining a vigil twenty-four hours a day. At 3:00 a.m. Tim found Allen on his knees in the middle of the hotel ballroom deeply entrenched in prayer. The image of the mountain of a man postured humbly on his knees testifies of Allen's deep commitment to God and constant support of his friends.

Eventually Tim and Father Spitzer decided to reimagine their efforts to help strengthen people's faith. They started the Magis Institute, a non-profit educational organization dedicated to uniting disciplines like physics, philosophy, and reason with faith. They wanted to create a curriculum to help fortify high school and college students with the tools to intellectually defend their faith in secular academic spaces often dominated by new age atheistic ideas. They approached Allen with the idea and he helped them organize a Board of Directors and secure the necessary funding. Allen would serve on the board and invite the members to Long Canyon Ranch for a retreat.

Allen was so excited to have Father Spitzer at the ranch. He deeply respected the wealth of wisdom Father Spitzer supplied and Allen opened up to him in ways he didn't with other people. They enjoyed a special friendship. Father Spitzer was afflicted with a condition that was rapidly causing his vision to deteriorate. So Allen took great care to describe in vivid detail the views at the ranch. He would paint an oral picture of the specific hues of pinks and purples that streaked across the sky and melted together at sunset, and the way the cliffs scattered deep shadows on the earth below. His words dripped with such striking detail, Father Spitzer could see it all in his mind's eye. Whether creating a mental picture for him or guiding him to climb on the back of a four wheeler, Allen was determined to make sure Father Spitzer never felt left out of any experience the group embarked on at the ranch.

The ranch was a gift Allen could give to people, and on this occasion Father Spitzer would give Allen something in return: a new way of seeing God that required, not natural, but spiritual sight. During their conversations, Allen loved to talk about new projects they could do to share their faith with the world, and what they could endeavor to build together. However, on this day Father Spitzer stopped and asked Allen if he had ever taken time to contemplate who God was and how much God loved him apart from anything he could do to serve Him. He noticed how Allen always seemed busy "working for God" and wondered if Allen ever slowed down long enough to simply receive God's love. The conversation caught Allen off guard. Time focused on receiving from God sounded selfish, and contemplation was more in Kathie's wheelhouse, so Allen usually left that to her.

"Have you considered how much God loves you, Allen? And perhaps what He wants to do for you, rather than what you're trying to do for Him?" Father Spitzer asked.

"I think that's more of Kathie's thing," Allen replied lightly.

"That's right," Father Spitzer continued, "And that is why she is a great complement to you, Allen. But she also has great inner peace. For all you have done, I wonder how much was done from a place of peace, of connection to God versus an obligation to Him. Do you let God love you?"

"Don't I owe it to God after saving me from the wildfire?" Allen asked. He still had recurring dreams of the event that changed the course of his life.

Allen admitted, "Sometimes I'm afraid everything I've built is going to burn up like that bulldozer tomorrow. And sometimes I worry I haven't done enough."

Father Spitzer was convinced that wildfire was the ignition spark that caused Allen Lund to take off like a rocket, determined to hold up his end of the bargain to live for God. Yet the reason we can live for God is because Jesus died for us. The reason we can love God is because He first loved us, while we were all still running from him. Father Spitzer wondered if perhaps Allen's complicated relationship with his own biological father made it difficult to conceptualize God as a loving Heavenly Father.

"Have you ever considered," Father Spitzer pondered, "that perhaps the reason He pulled you out of that fire was simply because He loved you, and that perhaps He just wanted you to know Him and be able to receive His love?"

The question brought tears to Allen's eyes. It was easier to serve than it was to receive, but God's grace and love couldn't be achieved or earned; they could only be accepted as the free gifts that they are. From that day forward, Allen began to think about what it meant to allow God to love him, reflecting that his value to God had nothing to do with the amount he could do for Him. Still, Allen was more comfortable giving than he was receiving. This was true in his family and friendships as well.

Allen never wanted anyone to make a fuss over him. This was especially true as his age started to catch up with him. Allen had to have two knee replacement surgeries, and while prepping for the second surgery the doctor discovered a murmur in his heartbeat. This necessitated triple bypass surgery. Allen fully recovered from all of these setbacks. He was a hearty man who fought to stay active and bounced back from things quickly.

This is why his family became concerned after Allen took a bad fall at the ranch in July 2017. He attempted to dislodge a large pipe when it suddenly broke and caused him to fall backwards. The result was a compression fracture in his back. Allen wasn't bouncing back from this injury as he had others. He wasn't able to be as active and needed to sit a lot more. At first the family thought it was just the injury, but they began to suspect other things were at play since Allen dropped a lot of weight and had little appetite. His blood pressure was also inconsistent and Allen started to fall more often.

The Lunds tried to find out what was happening. Allen juggled a myriad of doctors. He had an eye infection which wouldn't go away. He was having issues with memory and occasional confusion. He was also sleeping a lot more than usual. For months no one could put all of the medical pieces together. But at the end of February 2018, Allen's doctor ordered three MRIs and bloodwork which revealed cancer in Allen's liver. By this point Allen's health had rapidly deteriorated and he had very little strength. His family were looking at a shell of the physically-imposing man they were used to seeing barrelling down the hallways at the ALC building or hopping aboard one of his machines at Long Canyon. Allen called each of his children individually to tell them about the diagnosis. More tests would be required for further specifics, and he knew he would need to be admitted to the hospital soon for a biopsy of his liver. To prepare for the procedure the doctors took Allen off of all medications. Allen needed to wait a few weeks for the medication to get out of his system and for his body to stabilize before he would be ready for the procedure. However, Allen was also determined to wait to undergo the biopsy until after his granddaughter's wedding in March. He wanted to be there, and he didn't want his health issues to be a distraction from the felicity of the festivities.

The week of his diagnosis was also the week of the annual managers meeting at the ALC corporate office. Allen wanted so badly to be there, but his health was too poor to attend.

Instead, he decided to call into the meeting to speak to the managers. Allen didn't want to video call, because he didn't want his change in appearance to alarm anyone. The managers knew Allen wasn't doing well, and although Allen had every intention of fighting this cancer, a somber understanding hung like heavy drapes in the meeting room; this may be the last time Allen would speak to them. Kathie watched her husband use all of his energy to make his voice clear and strong on the phone. Kenny put the call on the sound system so everyone in the room could hear what turned out to be their last directives. Allen told them they were the best employees in the entire world, and how blessed he felt to work with all of them. He also made one request: that they continue the tradition of the Acts of Kindness because it is so important to give back. His speech was short and to the point, but extremely heartfelt. There wasn't a single person in the room who wasn't crying. Allen's employees loved him not just as a leader, but also as a man.

Allen attended his granddaughter's wedding on March 24, 2018 and the festivities continued the following day as the family celebrated the beginning of Holy Week. They gathered at Kenny and Mary's house for Palm Sunday. They celebrated the holiday by holding palm branches and marching around the house together as a family. Allen watched them from the back porch, sitting next to his newly wed granddaughter, Ashley, who also couldn't join the march because she hurt her knee dancing at the wedding. The two enjoyed a private moment together, smiling as the family paraded. Allen quietly said, "I so wish you and I could get out there and join them."

Allen attended the 5:30 a.m. sunrise Mass on Easter Morning, which was hosted each year in the church parking lot. The pastor, Father Gerard O'Brian, knew Allen was struggling so he brought the Holy Communion to the window of his Ford Explorer. The following morning, April 2, 2018 Allen got up, showered, dressed himself, and rode to the hospital. His vitals were unstable and more tests were run to get a fuller understanding of the medical crisis he was facing. They concluded Allen had bile duct cancer. Initially doctors were optimistic. Allen still seemed robust to them and they discussed various treatment plans with Kathie and the family. They admitted him to the hospital. Doctors wanted to stabilize him and administer the first round of chemotherapy the following day. However, they were less optimistic when they discovered Allen's kidneys had shut down and he would need dialysis to stay alive. His daughter Christina wanted to spend the night with him at the hospital Monday and Tuesday, but Allen wouldn't let her. He made it clear he wanted her to go home, be with her family, and not make a fuss over him. His voice was weak by this point so he ended the discussion by pointing at Christina and then emphatically pointing at the door.

Mary Lund, Kenny's wife, is a physical therapist and has

worked around the medical community her entire career. She sat with Kathie patiently translated the information the doctors were providing. Elaine Boggess, a nurse and friend of the family also came to offer Kathie additional counsel. The doctors were no longer confident Allen's body could sustain the cancer treatment, since his kidneys were no longer functioning properly. Dialysis would keep Allen alive longer, but it was unlikely he would ever leave the hospital. Although Allen was conscious for all these discussions, the decision ultimately lay with Kathie on what she felt was best.

On Wednesday morning, Kathie told the doctors she wanted to take Allen home. When she explained to Allen they were going to discharge him, he looked around the hospital room and said, "All of this technology and all of these brilliant doctors and no one can fix me." He found Christina's eyes.

"So they're gone-zo?" Allen asked. Christina nodded her head. Allen muttered, "I know what that means." He took a deep breath. For a moment everyone in the room was silent.

"Who would've thought the kidneys would take me out," he remarked, trying to keep things light. But a heavy realization had filled the room. Allen was facing death. He looked at Kenny and David, who were also there, and began to give them instructions. "Don't mess up the company" and "take care of Mom" were the general sentiments, but he also gave them a stream of consciousness list of details like passwords and locations of certain documents they would need. Everyone was grappling to come to terms with what was happening.

As soon as Kathie made the decision to take Allen home, everything pivoted. They began the process of getting Allen discharged. Hospice care was arranged to be administered at the house. Family members who had left Los Angeles on travels or to go back to school booked return flights. Friends were called. Father Matt Elshoff, Allen's best friend, was asked to come and celebrate Mass for the family when Allen arrived. An ambulance was arranged to take Allen home and the family pushed back all of the furniture in the living room to make room for Allen's hospital bed, because Kathie wanted him to be in a room where it was easy for people to visit him. Large numbers of people started showing up at the Lund house to greet Allen. Family and friends poured into the living room. Among them was a bishop, a cardinal, a priest, and eleven Carmelite Sisters, including Sister Regina Marie. Kathie stood outside directing traffic, as so many people were showing up. They still needed to have space for the ambulance to pull up to the front door.

Allen had no clue any of this was happening. He rode in the ambulance digesting the heavy reality in the solitude of his mind. So he was shocked when they wheeled him into his home to see the faces of so many people. He scanned the room, catching the glistening eyes of his many loved ones who showed up to be with him. Their reception touched his heart.

His face lit up with sheer delight and he opened his arms to greet them with a "Well, golly!" as if he had arrived at his own surprise birthday party. The love in the room was palpable as was the presence of God. Everyone prayed and wept together during a heartfelt Mass. The Carmelite Sisters sang and Father Matt gave the homily. The readings of the day seemed to relate perfectly to Allen's journey. Father Matt explained how when Jesus spoke about "His hour," he was referring to his passion, death, and resurrection.

Then Father Matt looked over to Allen and said, "This is your hour, Allen; this is your finest hour. This is the reason why you were baptized, why you and Kathie were married, why you participated in the sacraments for so many years. Look around you. Look at the fruit of your marriage and your faith. Your children and their children are all alive in Christ. Your friends are here with you because the love and faith of community strengthens us. We are entering into this moment with you because the Resurrection of Christ is meant for you, Allen. This is what life is all about. This is your finest hour."

The homily shifted everyone's hearts. The family realized they were witnessing the greatest days of their father's life, because he was never before so close to Heaven. Jesus died on a cross so that everyone who believes in Him will not perish, but have eternal life. This truth comforted them and supplied them with a peace that transcended their grief. Allen also shifted to allow his family to be with him in his hour. He didn't worry that they were fussing over him too much. He didn't shoo them away or ask them to go home. He let them stay close to him, desiring to cherish every moment he could with them.

After Mass, Allen asked for a hug from everyone there. They all formed a line to embrace him and exchange some loving words. Allen received each embrace wholeheartedly. His loved one's were like the hands and feet of Jesus comforting Allen on the Earth. They potently administered God's love as well as their own to Allen, lifting him up as he had always done for them. Their compassion helped Allen understand more about the powerful love of His Heavenly Father. Each hug was a foretaste of a greater embrace that Allen awaited, when he would soon go into the arms of his loving Savior.

As the crowd began to disperse, Allen was with his family. They gathered blankets and pillows to sleep on the floor around his bed. In the evening he told them he was hungry, so his daughters rushed into the kitchen to try to figure out something good for him to eat. They found a jar of Utah peaches that were canned and given to them by Allen's friend, Dennis, whose dental work Allen had paid for all those years ago. It's fitting that the sweetness of his life would accompany him near the time of his death. He enjoyed a few bites. Utah peaches and Holy Communion were the last things Allen would eat as his strength continued to fade over the next few days.

Grief was inseparably woven with immense gratitude in the Lund home. There was beauty, even in the midst of great difficulty. The immense love that surrounded Allen Lund as he wholeheartedly embraced his finest hour was, like the peaches, sweet evidence of a life well lived.

CHAPTER TWENTY-ONE

FINEST HOUR

"I have fought the good fight, I have finished the race, I have kept the faith."

—*2 Timothy 4:7*

Family life was fully in session in the Lund home during Allen's final days. There was a blessing in the timing of events. Many grandchildren had already come into town for Easter and were able to stay at their grandparent's home. Other family members and friends quickly booked flights to join them. They slept wherever they could find real estate on the living room floor surrounding Allen's bed. Getting up to check on him meant tip-toeing through a maze of sleeping bags. Emotionally, however, there was no tip-toeing around what was really happening. The Lunds embraced the pain and difficulty of death as wholeheartedly as they embraced their love and gratitude for Allen's life. The knowledge that these were Allen's final days made everyone cherish each moment more ardently. They wept together, laughed together, shared memories, and took turns holding Allen's hands.

Allen's children sat in the living room, their faces soaked in tears, praying the rosary with their own children snuggled on their laps. No one hid their pain, nor did they stifle their joy. Five minutes later they would share a funny story that made the whole room laugh, and the grandchildren would run outside to play. Prayers, crossword puzzles, songs, memories, meals, and children's games became like the threads of a great tapestry depicting a family never before more deeply connected than they were in that moment.

Friends poured into the home to say goodbye to Allen and those who couldn't make it sent letters to him which the family read aloud. Although Allen's strength was fading, he found ways to let his friends know he was glad to see them. When the Carmelite Sisters came back to visit Allen on Friday, he put his hand feebly to his lips and blew them a kiss. Steve Francom flew in from Utah to see Allen. When Steve walked in the door, Allen reached for him. When Allen's granddaughter, Katherine, told him she had decided to attend the University of Portland, Allen gave her an approving thumbs up. These were small ways Allen reminded his loved ones he was listening.

Allen approached his death as he had his life—with faith, joy, and humility. Allen believed no matter what life brought, God's love and the power of Jesus' crucifixion and resurrection would always prevail over all circumstances. This faith guarded his mind from worry his whole life and it blanketed the home with peace in the hour of his death. Allen was not afraid. He did not complain. Though his health waned, his joy remained unshaken. When his family asked how he was, he quietly replied, "I'm wonderful." Allen was so thankful to be surrounded by all the people he loved the most. He had always shown up on the sidelines of every game or major event of their lives. Now his family was doing the same for him.

That Friday night, Steve Francom shared many funny and touching stories about Allen on the ranch. Everyone gathered to listen. Steve needed to catch a plane back to Utah, so he said goodbye to the man who had become like a father to him. The family remained huddled together reflecting on Steve's words. He had shared things with them they never knew about Allen, specifically ways he had shown kindness to people. The family, touched and motivated by the way their father and grandfather poured his life out for others, decided to take turns expressing to Allen what they planned to do with their lives. They wished to carry on his legacy of doing as much good as they could for as many people as they could for as long as they could.

After they had all spoken, Allen used his remaining strength to utter, "Can you hear me? I love you all." Those words, faint but potent, would be Allen's last statement as his vitality continued to slip away.

Allen slept peacefully that night, but his family jumped up like prairie dogs every time there was a slight change in his breathing. Around 10:00 a.m. Saturday, Sister Regina Marie and a few other Carmelite Sisters stopped by the home again to offer prayers and encouragement. They had called ahead of time. So before their arrival, Kathie orchestrated a twenty minute quick clean up of the house. She also insisted her granddaughter's, many of whom were wearing Kathie's clothes, go brush their hair and look presentable before the Caramelites arrived. The Lunds were increasingly aware of just how little time Allen had left. No one wanted to leave the living room.

Everyone was ready when the Sisters arrived. Years serving in an acute hospital prepared the Carmelites to accompany people in their final hours. Sister Regina Marie sat next to her friend Allen. He had always been a beacon of strength for her whenever she needed encouragement or wisdom. Now she saw his fragility. His eyes were glazed and cloudy, and his jaw was locked ajar. She had seen these signs in other people nearing death. Sister Regina Marie called Kathie into the living room to be with them and asked the Lund children to form a circle in prayer around Allen. The Carmelite Sisters began to sing hymns and songs of blessing over Allen. As they sang "O Sacred Heart of Jesus, I Place My Trust In Thee," Allen's eyes became clear and his jaw, which had been locked in an open position, gently closed. The Sisters were stunned to see him look alert.

They continued singing their hymn, a sung prayer. It became the narration of this sacred moment.

The last verse of the song, which was aptly chosen, reads, "But most of all in that last hour, when death points up above. O Sweet Savior, may Thy face smile on my soul all free. Oh may I cry with rapturous love, I've placed my trust in Thee."

Allen looked up with clear eyes. His mouth opened again, this time in joyful awe of what he alone was seeing. He hadn't had the strength to move, but somehow miraculously he lifted his hands up toward heaven as if reaching for a hug from above. In that very moment, Allen gave up his spirit and breathed his last. His arms slowly floated back down and rested by his side. In the glistening of an eye, he passed from this life to the next. Sister Regina Marie asked someone to close his eyes. The family were still tightly holding hands, overcome with emotion. Eddie's friend Michael Betance stepped forward and gently brushed his hand over Allen's face, closing the eyes of his great mentor. Allen's eyelids were soft and supple like those of a child. His face was at peace and the family knew then that he was gone.

No one gathered there had ever seen a more beautiful death. Witnessing Allen step into eternal life strengthened their faith. There was no doubt in their minds that Saturday April 7, 2018 (The Vigil of the Feast of Divine Mercy) was the day Allen Lund looked up and saw the face of Jesus, his loving Savior, come to welcome him home.

The poet Megan Devine writes that "There are losses that rearrange the world."

One week later, Allen's funeral was hosted at the Cathedral of Our Lady of the Angels. The large sanctuary was filled with people coming to pay their respects to this mountain of a man who left a profound impact on the world. Friends, family, business leaders, and ALC employees filled the pews next to members of the Equestrian Order of the Holy Sepulchre of Jerusalem, the Order of St. Gregory, and the Equestrian Order of the Knights of Malta. Also present were the boards of St. Francis High School and University of Portland. The Carmelite Sisters formed a choir behind the altar, and Allen's family followed a processional to the front of the church led by twenty-one priests and the ArchBishop of Los Angeles. The vast array of attendees spoke to Allen's devotion to the Catholic Church and to his unique ability to make everyone he met feel like family.

The processional accompanied Allen's casket through the tall bronze doors at the entrance of the cathedral and processed down the center aisle of the church, an honor usually bestowed only upon clergy and dignitaries. Next to the altar adorned with white lillies was a framed photo of Allen in his cowboy hat leaning against the front of a semi-truck. His arms were confidently crossed and he bore a knowing smile. This was how many people remembered him. Allen's best friend, Father Matt Elshoff, led the Mass and gave the first homily. Father Mark

Poorman of the University of Portland also gave a heartfelt homily, and Allen's three sons shared stories expressing the depth of Allen's incredible life. Allen's grandchildren, Kevin and Noel, also spoke about what it was like to be a Lund grandchild, serving as representatives for all twenty-two of them.

The first reading selected for the Mass was from the Book of Genesis. It was the story of God calling Abraham to go to a new land where God promised to bless him, make of him a great nation, and make Abraham's name great so he could be a blessing to all the people on earth. There couldn't have been a more fitting scripture for the funeral of Allen Lund. The parallels between Allen and Abraham's lives are striking. They both moved to new places, trusting God to provide for their families. Their journeys began with a promise, and they took God at his word. Abraham's faith enabled him to inherit a blessing that radiated to all the nations on earth. And in his own way, Allen too inherited a blessing that would impact generations. The more success God gave Allen, the greater he was able to be a blessing to those around him. The evidence of this blessing were sitting in the pews of the church; people whose lives were touched by the love of Allen Lund.

During the service Allen's grandchildren carried keepsakes down the center aisle to place around Allen's picture. There were photographs of his building projects, his boots and cowboy hat, his baseball and glove, antlers from the last deer he got hunting, a folded American flag, his work shirt, a Caterpillar trucker cap, a book of crossword puzzles, and more. Each item reflected the multi-faceted life of terrific accomplishment he led.

A question those closest to Allen often ask is how was he able to accomplish so much. Where did he find the time? What was his secret? When taking an audit of his life, the answer comes back to one resounding theme: God. Allen's life was planted in the earth the day he surrendered it to God in that wildfire; a seed which brought forth a beautiful harvest. God does not look for the best leaders, the most capable, or most accomplished, he searches for hearts yielded to Him. God can do anything with a life that is wholly His. Allen sought after God every day and considered the Bible the best management book ever written because it teaches how to love and uplift others.

In true Allen Lund fashion, the funeral Mass ended with the singing of "God Bless America." His family gathered around his casket and his children reached out their hands to touch it one last time before the pallbearers carried him to the burial. The Lund Family gave each pallbearer a pocket knife, because Allen always carried one. Engraved on the side of each blade were the words "Get to Work."

The message was clear: It's now our turn to be the stewards of Allen Lund's legacy. Allen's family and friends share the same sentiment: a desire to make Allen proud and continue the good works he started. They feel they are all stepping into a big man's shadow. However, despite how others saw him, Allen never considered himself a giant of industry, faith, or anything else. He simply distilled life's big picture into a simple credo: Go to church, work hard, and be good.

During the homily, Father Matt referred to Allen as a "middle class saint," an ordinary person who led with integrity, sought good for others, and showed up heroically in his life. The lesson was that everyone has the power to do the same. When everyday people seek God's goodness in their lives, God's grace builds on their own particular natures to accomplish great things. In this instance, God used a country boy from northern Utah with boots and a trucker hat to bring many people to faith.

After his death, the Lunds heard many stories of Allen's kindness, encouragement, and radical generosity; things they never knew their father did for people. There were also several people who decided to join the Catholic Church, and many others who recommitted themselves to weekly Mass attendance. They were inspired by Allen's faith, and they wanted to find what he found. Allen's most beautiful legacy is that his sons, daughters, and grandchildren all know God. Love of God and love for each other has sealed the Lunds with a mighty bond.

Throughout the preparations, the rosary, visitation, and funeral, Kathie Lund, Allen's widow, stood like a pillar of strength adorned with a quiet peacefulness that transcended understanding. Allen loved Kathie since the summer nights he spent sleeping on a park bench outside of the cashier's office at Lagoon Amusement Park. He'd stay outside until she was done counting the money just so he could walk her safely to her car. He was smitten and stayed that way for fifty-seven years. Allen was quiet around Kathie the final week of his life. It's hardest to say goodbye to those we love the most. She understood, knowing him better than anyone. Kathie carries on Allen's legacy as she continues to be the hub of family life, good works, and adventure.

A year after saying goodbye to her best friend and husband, Kathie went on another study tour of Israel. The trip had spiritual and emotional significance since she had previously gone there with Allen. Kathie sat on a bench overlooking the Sea of Galilee, a tranquil place untouched by time. The fresh waters lapped against a shoreline of pebbles and reeds. There Kathie sat and reflected on many things. Suddenly she experienced an intense buzzing heat that started in her chest and radiated upward to the top of her head. She had never felt anything like it before and didn't understand what was happening until her heart heard an undeniable message.

"You know I always loved you," he said.

Tears filled Kathie's eyes as she replied, "I know, I've always known. I'm fine. Go take care of everyone else."

The moment fled as suddenly as it came, but it left Kathie with a feeling she will cherish in her heart forever. Her request was answered. Many of Allen's relatives and friends feel they now have an extra person praying for them in Heaven. They think about the lessons Allen taught them and wonder how often he leans over the rails of heavenly bleachers, cheering them on as he did all those years watching their baseball games, graduations, skits, and concerts.

Only now, Allen Lund cheers on all of us, as we participate in the race of life. The principles of his life encourage us to fight the good fight of faith and finish strong the race set out before us by doing as much good and uplifting as many people as we can with the time we are given.

Death for a Christian isn't really a goodbye, and Allen never said goodbye anyway. We close as he would, with directives simple and profound.

Go to church. Get to work. And always remember: Be Good.

A FEW WORDS FROM
THE EMPLOYEES OF ALLEN LUND COMPANY

Allen was a fun but also very principled and honorable man in a highly competitive industry. That took a rare strength of personality.

Rich Rathbun, 21 years with ALC
Cargo Claim Administrator

If you were in a room with Allen, he wasn't the loudest or most talkative person there. Sometimes you might even think he wasn't paying attention. But then he would say something that made you realize he had heard everything and processed everything, and his statements were powerful, insightful, and interesting. He was calculative in that way and only spoke when he had something to say.

Jim McGuire, 27 years with ALC
Executive Vice President

In business, Allen was a man who drove a hard bargain and did it the right way every day. Personally, he was a man who didn't waver in the priorities of his family, his country, and God.

Jim Scazzero, 32 years with ALC
General Manager, Atlanta, GA

I had an employee whose husband had a tragic accident and passed away. Allen called me and asked me what he could do for her. He offered to pay for the entire funeral. He did pay for it and got loyalty from that employee that will never go away.

Chris Clelland, 29 years with ALC
General Manager, Flatbed Office

He donated two hundred fifty dollars in memory of my grandmother at our local hospice. I had only been hired on for a month. It was pretty special.

Jon Manning, 8 years with ALC
General Manager, Cincinnati, OH

Allen was larger than life, in both his physical stature and his incredible character. Within 5 minutes of speaking to him a person would be able to discern his staunch integrity, his inspiring common sense, and the fact that he didn't mince words in a conversation on almost any subject. He was one of the most truthful and up front people I've ever known and he was the most real person I've ever met. His Catholic values, though not trumpeted, were evident in the way he led our company, in the constant integrity he displayed to everyone, and the compassion he showed to his employees and others.

Steve Asip, 38 years with ALC
Retired General Manager & Board Member

His best piece of advice: Take care of your people.

Matt Gronostaj, 20 years with ALC
General Manager, Memphis, TN

Citizens Bank, catty-corner from the office, had been robbed, and the thieves had taken off on foot and were scrambling around in our parking lot looking for a place to hide. Allen grabbed one of Eddie's Dodger baseball bats and chased them under a car where he held them at bay until the cops arrived! He had his game face on, was ready for battle if need be, and was determined to not let them get away. He was keeping his employees and the whole community safe.

Tracey Lewin, 37 years with ALC
Vice President of Sales and Operations

He was as big as life—generous, kind, but tough when necessary.

Nora Trueblood, 22 years with ALC
Director of Marketing

I have great memories of him always walking in the office to say hi and to see how everyone was doing. It would always make me smile and he knew how to make you laugh on the days that you needed it.

Kirsten Brodie, 26 years with ALC
Manager of the Customer Service Center

Once I was walking by his office and he had a priest visiting, he called out to me to come in and introduced us. He continued to share with the priest that I volunteered with a Grief Group at my church. I could not believe that he remembered that about me, and that he wanted to share it with this person. As I left his office, I felt like he was proud of me, and he said, "Keep helping others, that is our most important job here on Earth."

Pamela Koerber, 12 years with ALC
Human Resources Coordinator

Many years ago my Father-in-Law was in a tragic accident. I called Mr Lund looking for my Husband (he worked for him). When I told Mr. Lund what had happened he immediately jumped into action. He drove out to Arcadia and picked up my mother-in-law and drove her down to USC. He stayed with us for hours. His kindness made a terrible situation more bearable.

Deann Saar, 32 years with ALC
Manager of Carrier Resources

I really love that the company's Act of Kindness initiative was such an important priority of his. He really wanted to be sure it continued when he was gone. I think that says a lot about the kind of person Allen was.

Bob Rose, 39 years with ALC,
Vice President

He was great, and he gave you the opportunity to work with good people.

Al Leiker, 10 years with ALC
Retired General Manager

He told me on day one when I was with him in the LA office, I would be successful if I worked hard, was honest and fair. It was a simple formula and it really worked.

Bill Bess, 40+ years with ALC
Board Member, General Manager, Orlando, FL
"Big Al" Truck Driver

My second interview was with Allen and Bill Bess and I did not think it went very well with either of them. Fortunately for me, they decided to give me a chance, and I was offered a job in Orlando. I have tried my best to follow the company mantra of Customer, Company, Office and treat everyone with the utmost respect. Doing the right thing, even though it might be painful, is the Lund Way and things will work out in the end. The opportunities that have been made available to me have kept me with ALC all these years. They have also provided me with the ability to provide for my family and I will be forever grateful to Mr Lund.

Shaun Leiker, 30 years with ALC
Manager, KS Freight

Allen was someone almost anyone could look up to, literally and figuratively. He spoke of how proud he was of all of us there and how special we were, and we believed him. He built my confidence. He inspired me. He 'sold' ALC to me, but without selling. It was a turning point for me. I often say joining ALC was the luckiest thing I ever did. Allen was and still is a role model of mine.

Ryan Stephenson, 17 years with ALC
Senior Director of Sales

One of my favorite days of the year was February 14, when Allen would walk through the building and give every gal in head-quarters a box of chocolate-covered caramels from his favorite candy shop in Utah. More important than the chocolate was the fun interaction with Allen.

Lori Gardner, 11 years with ALC
Executive Office Manager

Allen gave me an opportunity to open an office and gave me the autonomy to do it my way. When Hurricane Harvey hit Houston in 2017, I didn't know how I was going to be able to make things work, but Allen ensured me not to worry and said they would support me during the difficult time.

Michael Keep, 8 years with ALC
General Manager, Houston, TX

Thank you, Mr. Lund, for generating a pathway for shippers, truckers, and brokers to work together!

Katy Knight, 4 years with ALC
Senior Carrier Coordinator

One of the last times I saw him, I told him he set an incredible high bar for my son's future employers. They grew up under his leadership, his kindness and this family example he set and they will expect their future companies/employers to be the same and I said they'd be in for quite a shock some day. He said two things. One, then they should come work here! and then, two, if not, then he hoped they found some place just like ALC.

Mike Terry, 22 years with ALC
Director of Project Management

While I was still a contractor for the company, my girlfriend and I were invited to the corporate Christmas party. During the trip, I proposed to my girlfriend. Allen heard that we had gotten engaged, and during his address to the party, he thanked me for my service to the company, then announced my engagement and congratulated us. We are still married today, and I feel like Allen gave us a little extra blessing in our marriage.

Bryan Wolford, 17 years with ALC
Manager of IT Support

SELECTED SOURCES

1. "Allen Lund Funeral Mass" YouTube, uploaded by Cathedral of Our Lady Of the Angels, Date Uploaded April 14, 2018, https://youtu.be/GKJThjBk-cuY?si=i-_xdWgTlvL9_JkJ. Accessed May 15, 2024.
2. The Bible. New International Version, Biblica, 2011.
3. Lewis, C.S. The Four Loves. Harcourt Brace Jovanovich, 1960.
4. "Allen Lund Company Mourns the Loss of a Leader: Allen Lund." *American Journal of Transportation*, https://www.ajot.com/news/allen-lund-company-mourns-the-loss-of-a-leader-allen-lund. Accessed 7 May 2024.
5. "Allen and Kathleen Lund honor family, faith, and formation with a new gift to the University." *University of Portland News*, https://www.up.edu/news/2016/05/allen-kathleen-lund-new-gift.html. Accessed 7 May 2024.
6. "Allen Lund Passes Away." *University of Portland News*, https://www.up.edu/news/2018/04/allen-lund-passes-away.html. Accessed 7 May 2024.
7. "Best Charles Spurgeon Quotes: 21 Outstanding Sayings." What Christians Want to Know, n.d., https://www.whatchristianswanttoknow.com best-charles-spurgeon-quotes-21-outstanding-sayings/.
8. "Bishop dedicates Saint Joseph Catholic Church." San Juan Record, 22 Nov. 2019, https://sjrnews.com/life-san-juan-monticello/bishop-dedicates-saint-joseph-catholic-church.
9. "Father Spitzer." Magis Center, https://www.magiscenter.com/father-spitzer.
10. "About Legatus." *Legatus*, https://legatus.org/legatus. Accessed 15 May 2024.
11. Miller, Roger. "Roger Miller Quotes." BrainyQuote, 2024, https://www.brainyquote.com/quotes/roger_miller_391942.
12. Okumura, Jordan. "Ride to the Top." The Snack, issue 11, June 2015, pp. 52-57.
13. "About Our Lady of the Angels Cathedral." Our Lady of the Angels Cathedral, https://olacathedral.org.
14. "About St. Francis High School." St. Francis High School, https://www.sfhs.net.
15. "Saint Joseph Catholic Church—Monticello." Diocese of Salt Lake City, https://www.dioslc.org/parishes/saint-joseph-catholic-church-monticello.
16. "St. Joseph Parish in Monticello breaks ground for new." iCatholic, Roman Catholic Diocese of Salt Lake City, 30 Oct. 2019, http://icatholic.dioslc.org/article/st-joseph-parish-in-monticello-breaks-ground-for-new-9276846.
17. "Allen and Kathleen Lund Honor Family, Faith, and Formation with a New Gift to the University." *University of Portland News*, https://www.up.edu/news/2016/05/allen-kathleen-lund-new-gift.html. Accessed 7 May 2024.
18. "10 Spurgeon Quotes on Dying Well." *The Spurgeon Center*, https://www.spurgeon.org/resource-library/blog-entries/10-spurgeon-quotes-on-dying-well/.

Accessed 9 May 2024.

19. "10 Quotes from John Paul II to Encourage Catholic School Educators." *EpicPew*, https://epicpew.com/10-quotes-from-john-paul-ii-encourage-catholic-school-educators/. Accessed 1 May 2024.

20. "45 Inspirational Dolly Parton Quotes to Live By." Country Living, Hearst Magazine Media, Inc., n.d., https://www.countryliving.com/life/entertainment/g4017/dolly-parton-quotes/#:~:text="I%20always%20count%20my%20blessings,for%20money%2C%20never%20did."

21. Reagan, Ronald "Actor, Ideologue, Politician: The Public Speeches of Ronald Reagan", Greenwood Publishing Group, 1993

22. Roosevelt, Franklin D. "White House Radio Address." Delivered at the White House, Washington, D.C., 5 Oct. 1944.

23. Roosevelt, Theodore. "Citizenship in a Republic." Delivered at the Sorbonne, Paris, France, 23 Apr. 1910.

24. Clapp, Anna. "Lund Family Meeting" Ongoing Interviews conducted by Jenna Day, November 2023—June 2024, Remote.

25. Lund-Doefler, Christina. "Lund Family Meeting" Ongoing Interviews conducted by Jenna Day, November 2023—June 2024, Remote.

26. Lund, David. "Lund Family Meeting" Ongoing Interviews conducted by Jenna Day, November 2023—June 2024, Remote.

27. Lund, Edward. "Lund Family Meeting" Ongoing Interviews conducted by Jenna Day, November 2023—June 2024, Remote.

28. Lund, Kathie. "Lund Family Meeting" Ongoing Interviews conducted by Jenna Day, November 2023—June 2024, Remote.

29. Lund, Kenneth. "Lund Family Meeting" Ongoing Interviews conducted by Jenna Day, November 2023—June 2024, Remote.

30. Peterson, Natalie. "Lund Family Meeting" Ongoing Interviews conducted by Jenna Day, November 2023—June 2024, Remote.

31. Amador, Philip. Interview. 11 Aug. 2022. Conducted by Anthony Preston.

32. Beauchamp, Fr. William. Interview. 13 May 2024. Conducted by Jenna Day.

33. Betance, Michael. Interview. 14 Oct. 2022. Conducted by Anthony Preston.

34. Bess, Bill. Interview. 14 Sep. 2021. Conducted by Anthony Preston.

35. Borzelliere, Craig. Interview. 15 Mar. 2024. Conducted by Jenna Day.

36. Busch, Tim. Interview. 11 Jan. 2025. Conducted by Jenna Day.

37. Clapp, Caroline. Personal interview. 17 Apr. 2024. Conducted by Jenna Day.

38. Clapp, Colleen. Personal interview. 17 Apr. 2024. Conducted by Jenna Day.

39. Clapp Huff, Allison. Personal interview. 17 Apr. 2024. Conducted by Jenna Day.

40. Clapp, James. Personal interview. 17 Apr. 2024. Conducted by Jenna Day.

41. Corrao, Deacon Tom. Interview. 15 Mar. 2024. Conducted by Jenna Day.

42. Doefler, Steve. Interview. 22 Jan. 2024. Conducted by Jenna Day.

43. Doerfler, Dean. Personal interview. 17 Apr. 2024. Conducted by Jenna Day.

44. Doerfler, Matthew. Personal interview. 17 Apr. 2024. Conducted by Jenna Day.

45. Doerfler, Ryan. Personal interview. 17 Apr. 2024. Conducted by Jenna Day.

46. Doerfler, Steve. Personal interview. 3 Jan. 2025. Conducted by Jenna Day.
47. Elshoff, Bishop Matthew. Interview. 5 June 2024. Conducted by Jenna Day.
48. Eulalia, Emmanuel. Interview. 18 Apr. 2024. Conducted by Jenna Day.
49. Francom, Steve. Interview. 15 Mar. 2024. Conducted by Jenna Day.
50. Gorman, Sister Regina Marie. Interview. 29 Apr. 2024. Conducted by Jenna Day.
51. Holtkamp, Judy. Interview. 11 Aug. 2022. Conducted by Anthony Preston.
52. Lewin, Tracey. Personal interview. 7 Jan. 2025. Conducted by Jenna Day.
53. Letchenberg-Durr, June. Interview. 26 May 2022. Conducted by Anthony Preston.
54. Lowe, Roger and Mary. Interview. 8 Mar. 2022. Conducted by Anthony Preston.
55. Lund Herrera, Katherine. Personal interview. 10 Apr. 2024. Conducted by Jenna Day.
56. Lund Prior, Ashley. Personal interview. 10 Apr. 2024. Conducted by Jenna Day.
57. Lund Rejsek, Clare. Personal interview. 10 Apr. 2024. Conducted by Jenna Day.
58. Lund, Alicia. Interview. 2 Nov. 2022. Conducted by Anthony Preston.
59. Lund, Elizabeth. Personal interview. 10 Apr. 2024. Conducted by Jenna Day.
60. Lund, Joseph. Personal interview. 10 Apr. 2024. Conducted by Jenna Day.
61. Lund, Mary. Interview. 3 Nov. 2022. Conducted by Anthony Preston.
62. Lund, Megan. Personal interview. 10 Apr. 2024. Conducted by Jenna Day.
63. Lund, Michael. Personal interview. 10 Apr. 2024. Conducted by Jenna Day.
64. Lund, Sarah. Personal interview. 10 Apr. 2024. Conducted by Jenna Day.
65. Lund, Thomas. Personal interview. 10 Apr. 2024. Conducted by Jenna Day.
66. McGuire, Jim. Personal interview. 13 Jan. 2025. Conducted by Jenna Day.
67. Lund Thomas, Kayla. Personal interview. 10 Apr. 2024. Conducted by Jenna Day.
68. Moran, Tom. Interview. 15 Apr. 2024. Conducted by Jenna Day.
69. Palmer, Tom. Interview. 15 Mar. 2024. Conducted by Jenna Day.
70. Peterson, Collin. Personal interview. 17 Apr. 2024. Conducted by Jenna Day.
71. Peterson, Kevin. Personal interview. 17 Apr. 2024. Conducted by Jenna Day.
72. Peterson, Kyle. Personal interview. 17 Apr. 2024. Conducted by Jenna Day.
73. Peterson Drew, Noel. Personal interview. 17 Apr. 2024. Conducted by Jenna Day.
74. Peterson Squiers, Madelyn. Personal interview. 17 Apr. 2024. Conducted by Jenna Day.
75. Poorman, Fr. Mark. Interview. 3 Nov. 2022. Conducted by Anthony Preston.
76. Romano, Tom. Interview. 16 Mar. 2022. Conducted by Anthony Preston.
77. Rose, Bob. Personal interview. 10 Jan. 2025. Conducted by Jenna Day.
78. Sciarappa, Lenny. Personal interview. 7 Jan. 2025. Conducted by Jenna Day.
79. Snashall, Kathleen. Interview. 15 Dec. 2022. Conducted by Anthony Preston.
80. Snashall, Mark. Interview. 1 Dec. 2022. Conducted by Anthony Preston.
81. Spitzer, Fr. Robert. Interview. 11 Aug. 2022. Conducted by Anthony Preston.
82. Spitzer, Fr. Robert. Interview. 17 June 2024. Conducted by Jenna Day
83. Tandon, Chetan. Interview. 27 Mar. 2024. Conducted by Jenna Day.
84. Wilcox, Ralph. Interview. 9 Aug. 2022. Conducted by Anthony Preston.

ABOUT THE AUTHOR

Jenna Day spent over a year researching and interviewing people who knew Allen Lund to paint a fitting portrait of a great man's life. Allen's life was multi-faceted and full of divine appointments. This is something Jenna knows all too well. A Miss America contestant turned actress and filmmaker, her work has been recognized internationally, awarded, and accepted to Oscar-qualifying film festivals. A chance meeting in Karachi Pakistan and another in a coffee shop in Studio City California led her to write books for inspiring people. Jenna is also the author of the Spiritual Haul Podcast, an exploration of the Bible that aims to bring people closer to God. She hopes readers will be as inspired by Allen's story as she was, and will ultimately find themselves encouraged to take meaningful action in their own lives.

ADDITIONAL RESEARCH AND CONTRIBUTIONS

Anthony W. Preston is an actor, producer, and host most notably known for his roles on daytime television shows such as "Days Of Our Lives," and "Young And The Restless." Anthony became passionate about providing resources for those wanting to improve their physical, mental, and spiritual health. He is a fitness brand ambassador and motivational speaker who creates resources and fitness journals to help people reach their goals. After Allen Lund funded one of Anthony's philanthropic endeavors, Anthony was eager to learn more about this generous benefactor. Anthony conducted and compiled research from interviews with Allen's friends and colleagues—a valued contribution to a book about a man he admired so greatly.